11.50
AF746866

SOUTH

WITHDRAWN

LOCAL-EXTERNAL ECONOMIES FOR BRITISH MANUFACTURING INDUSTRY

Local-External Economies for British Manufacturing Industry

P. M. TOWNROE

N. J. ROBERTS

University of East Anglia

Gower

© P. M. Townroe and N. J. Roberts 1980

All rights reserved. No part of this publication may be reproduced, stored in a retrieval system, or transmitted in any form or by any means, electronic, mechanical, photocopying, recording, or otherwise without the prior permission of Gower Publishing Company Limited.

British Library Cataloguing in Publication Data

Townroe, Peter Michael
Local - external economics for the British manufacturing industry.
1. Industries, Location of - Great Britain
2. Efficiency, Industrial - Great Britain
I. Title II. Roberts, N J
338.6'042 HC 260.D5

Published by
Gower Publishing Company Limited
Westmead, Farnborough, Hampshire, England

ISBN 0 566 00391 0

SOUTHAMPTON UNIVERSITY LIBRARY

Printed in Great Britain by
Biddles Ltd, Guildford, Surrey

Contents

Tables and figures

Table

Table

Figure

Figure

Appendix

Preface

This study has been made possible by the availability of a special data set from the 1968 Census of Production. This provided information on net output per head by industrial product group and by region and subregion in the United Kingdom. Using these figures, with all of their limitations, we have tried to investigate the extent to which the locational environment of a group of industrial plants in a given industrial sector influences the relative performance and efficiency of those plants. The results show significant differences between different sectors of industry and between the different sources of local external economy we have identified. The definition and the quantification of economies of agglomeration has been a major problem area for applied research in regional economics. We hope that this work will be useful in the continuing argument as to the significance of these economies.

Preliminary results of the study were published in an article: 'Externalities for Manufacturing Industry in British Subregions' (Townroe, 1979). This book reports the development of those results, made possible by a grant for nine man months of research time. Both authors have now been forced to move on to other interests but we hope that our efforts will encourage others to build on our results.

We have to acknowledge with thanks the assistance of the Business Statistics Office in the preparation of the original data set on which the dependent variables are based. We also have to thank Professor Michael Chisholm of the University of Cambridge and Professor Morgan Sant of the University of New South Wales for making available to us subregional data on which many of the independent variables were based.

We would also like to thank our colleague Richard Crum for most diligently reading the manuscript and making very useful suggestions. Responsibility for any errors of course remains with us. Thanks are also due to Carol Rodulfo for computing assistance and Mary Gurteen for typing.

The research was supported financially by the Research Fund of the School of Economic and Social Studies of the University of East Anglia; and by the Social Science Research Council under grant number HR 6279.

Peter M. Townroe
Nigel J. Roberts

University of East Anglia
Norwich
June 1980

1 Introduction

Economists have frequently been taken to task over the years by geographers, urban planners, transportation engineers and the like for ignoring space as a key variable in the explanation of economic behaviour. Considerable strides have now been made to remedy this alleged lack of interest. Over the past fifteen years or so, journals in urban and regional economics have appeared; most undergraduates have the option of taking relevant specialist courses; and the volume of published research seems to have been growing exponentially. Some workers in the field would claim that a new discipline has emerged, called 'Regional Science', which places the influence of space on social and economic behaviour at the centre of its interests.

However, amid this expanding academic activity, some important but basic theoretical and empirical questions remain unanswered. Urban and regional economics, like other specialist branches of the subject, is of course not alone in this. But one of the reasons for the neglect of space by economists was an assumption of its relative unimportance as a determinant in economic processes and hence as a key variable in economic models. This assumption has perhaps been particularly strong in the United Kingdom. The U.K. is spatially compact, with a good transportation infrastructure. Access from any one part of the country to any other is, by world standards, easy and cheap and there is little variation in the standard and availability of industrial infrastructure and public utilities from one part of the nation to another. The impression, or assumption, of the relative unimportance of space is strengthened when attention is paid to the behaviour of the productive sector of the economy by evidence of the low priority given to locational issues in industrial investment decisions within the United Kingdom (Townroe, 1971).

The location of industry and variations over space of the growth and performance of industry have however been an important focus for political debate and for policy formulation for many years in the United Kingdom. In particular, unemployment figures are recorded month by month for each locality. Any marked areal variation in these figures provides a strong political impetus to both regionally and locally based economic policies. The operation of these policies in turn provides an impetus to writing and research by economists.

One of the concerns thrown up by the arguments for regional economic development policies and by the difficulties involved in assessing their effectiveness and efficiency is a lack of knowledge of the significance of the <u>spatial</u> environment of a company or plant in manufacturing industry for the <u>efficiency</u> with which that company or plant is able to operate. Answers to the question of the relative efficiency by alternative location for a given industrial sector can be inferred by considering relative growth rates, usually in employment or output. But growth rates are indirect measures. Efficiency can be measured directly, although with difficulty. This book outlines an attempt to discover the significance of the spatial environment for the efficiency of industrial production processes directly, by associating alternative measures of efficiency with a variety of variables reflecting attributes of the spatial environment. The work has focussed on fifty-three sectors of manufacturing industry in sixty-one subregions of the United Kingdom in 1968.

This introductory chapter sets out the dimensions of the problem to be studied; it provides a little of the context of the study (although this is elaborated in later chapters); it states the aims of the work; and describes in outline the research methodology used. The final part of the chapter describes the contents of the nine subsequent chapters.

1 THE PROBLEM TO BE STUDIED

Externalities for manufacturing industry may be both positive and negative; they may be spatial and non-spatial; and they may operate at the level of the company or at the level of the individual factory, plant or process. Any given industrial activity will impose externality effects on other industrial activities and on the community at large; it will also be imposed upon itself by externality effects generated elsewhere in the economy. Some externality effects may be avoided; others are unavoidable.

This study is concerned with the influence of spatial relationships and location on industrial efficiency, where that efficiency is measured by the net output per employee and by two associated measures, allowing for regional variation in wage payments, and measuring total productivity of both labour and capital. It is concerned with both avoidable and unavoidable externalities which influence the relative levels of efficiency. The analysis has been undertaken at the spatial level of the subregion. The focus of the study is therefore on those externality effects which arise because of the location of the industrial establishment. Each establishment, or group of establishments, in a specified industrial sector within a given subregion operates within an external but local environment. This environment influences economic decisions and efficiency within the establishment or the sector. Although each establishment forms part of the local environment for every other establishment in the subregion, only those influences coming into the firm are considered here. Local externality effects such as smoke or noise pollution, imposed by an industrial operation on to other industrial activities and on to the rest of the community are not considered.

The local economic environment may influence the efficiency with which an industrial process may be operated and consequently the speed at which it may grow in a number of different ways. The most common influence will be by lowering costs. Easy local access to a range of suppliers of inputs and services will keep costs down, especially if there is strong competition between alternative suppliers. These costs may also be held down if the suppliers can experience economies of scale, perhaps available only on the basis of supplying a number of separate local companies. There is therefore an economy of agglomeration available to one specified industrial process or plant, available because the process or plant is located close by other processes or plants using similar inputs and services. Agglomerations of plants encourage the emergence of specialist suppliers. These suppliers can offer lower prices than suppliers elsewhere because they are local. They operate at a lower cost than our industrial firm can provide the input or service from within its own organisation because of technological specialisation and skill and economies of scale.

The local provision of inputs and services for some sectors may not result in lower costs as above, but rather it will result in higher profits. This is because the specialist suppliers provide a higher quality input than can be provided by the firm itself, resulting in an ability to charge a higher final product price. The increase in quality may also result from the industrial plant recruiting its labour force from a local labour pool, a pool which may have a long tradition, backed by a relevant local education and training infrastructure, in the skills relevant to the process in question. Demand considerations are also important here. For some firms and processes close contact with customers may be essential, requiring close proximity in a local area or subregion. For others, this local proximity may not be essential but it allows lower costs or higher prices.

Further advantages of agglomeration, those benefits arising from the local environment and proximity of a plant to other factories and offices, will include the more indirect consequences of a widening of available choice: of suppliers of inputs and services, of customers, of labour. An allied consequence for the company lies in being able to reduce uncertainty. Financial uncertainty can be reduced by purchasing-in components and services until the technology of a new process or the market for its output is established; and by renting or leasing rather than purchasing capital equipment. Uncertainty in recruiting key members of the labour force or in offering supply contracts is lessened if it is known that local alternatives exist.

All of these local influences upon industrial costs, profits and efficiency essentially arise because of the spatial juxtaposition of different industrial processes, suppliers, services and customers. They are all economies of agglomeration. These economies will be reflected in the local linkages between the various economic agencies. Some of these linkages involve the physical transfer of goods and components. Others are reflected in the transfer of skills or of information.

Some economies of agglomeration will be traded off against parallel diseconomies. For example, the benefits gained in the ways suggested above by a firm locating its factory in an urban area have to be set against possible higher land and utility costs, and higher wages to compensate the work force for commuting expenditures. This trade off makes the empirical identification of separate sources of agglomeration economy particularly difficult, and points to the advantage of considering the net output of plants as the residual return to labour and capital after other expenses have been met (although, as we shall see, the U.K. data is not completely unambiguous on this).

The problem to be studied is therefore the significance of spatial relationships in aggregate on the relative efficiency of a given industrial sector across subregions. The spatial relationships within companies, between the separate plants and offices where a company operates from more than one location, are not studied. Nor are the more dynamic aspects of agglomeration economies wherein the investment decisions of one company will influence the investment and growth of other companies located in the same area. Although the focus is on subregions, it must be remembered that some agglomeration economies may operate at higher orders of the regional hierarchy. The economies will almost certainly not operate to the boundaries of the subregions defined in advance for the study.

2 THE CONTEXT OF THE STUDY

The detailed intellectual heritage of this study is laid out in chapters two and three, particularly in chapter three where reference is made to the more important attempts to quantify the importance of agglomeration economies for manufacturing industry in developed economies. The realisation that a manufacturing company frequently performs better (i.e. is more profitable and grows faster) when located close by other manufacturing companies goes back of course to the experience of the second stage of the industrial revolution, when industrial processes were no longer tied tightly to sources of coal and water power. Rapidly growing industrial cities in the mid-nineteenth century, such as Manchester or Birmingham, demonstrated that different companies and different sectors of industry gained significant advantages in being linked closely one to another and in sharing services that were only economic when serving many people or many industrial concerns concurrently. In 1909, the German economist Alfred Weber formally recognised this importance of agglomeration in his Theory of the Location of Industries.

Since Weber, (and in particular since the 1929 publication of a translation of his work into English (Weber, 1929)), both urban geographers and the minority of economists who have concerned themselves with the significance of economic relationships over space have consistently referred to the importance of agglomeration economies in general terms. The term appears in most urban textbooks. The concepts of agglomeration and of local interindustry linkages are frequently used to help explain the evolution and growth of cities. The concepts are central to the idea of positive cumulative causation, a virtuous spiral of growth in the industrial development process.

Detailed empirical studies of agglomeration economies are harder to find than these general usages. Two broad approaches are possible. One is to seek to identify in a city or group of cities the presence of those factors, services or institutions which *a priori* reasoning has suggested contribute to economies of agglomeration. The second is to try to associate what are reasoned to be the results of these locational advantages in the relative success of an industry or industries in one location rather than another with the spatial patterning both of the production units and the related urban services etc. These two broad approaches to the understanding of agglomeration and linkage may be seen in four groups of studies, each group using a distinctive research method and focus.

The first group of studies have sought distinctive spatial associations between pairs and groups of industries. If an industry is strongly concentrated with many plants located in a single area or if plants in a pair of industrial sectors are frequently located within the same area, then it might be assumed that some form of advantageous interdependency exists between the plants or that the group of plants are benefitting from some general external economy. The principal danger behind this assumption and hence behind these aggregate studies is that a given locational pattern for an industry or group of industries may reflect the economic forces of yesterday rather than the locational pressures on a modern best practice technology plant. These studies are therefore useful in examining historical pressures, especially if changes in location are examined; but the current importance of agglomeration economies may be approached more directly by surveys of industrial plants, the second group of studies. Here, firms have been questioned on the pattern of their sales and purchase to find out the significance of the linkages with other concerns in the local area.

If the aim of research in this area is to discover the importance of agglomeration economies in a policy oriented normative sense, then the second group of studies is also weakened by inertia in the locational distribution of industrial plants. A complex of new industrial investments may choose a location which results in a distribution of sales and purchases quite different from that revealed in the general survey studies of plants old and new. A third group of studies therefore focusses on new investments, either by examining the locational distribution of investment seen in the growth of floorspace, capital stock, employment or output; or by surveying industrial plants recently established in new locations to discover their pattern of sales and purchases, or to discover which prospective external economies from the local area were important in determining the choice of location and site.

The present study builds on all of the three groups of agglomeration study briefly outlined above but it really belongs to a fourth group: studies which have tried to test whether spatial variations in the growth or level of productivity in industry, in aggregate or sector by sector, are associated with variations in the size or form of industrial agglomerations. In particular, it develops the work of

Brown (1972) who used values of net output per head by Standard Industrial Order for twelve regions in Great Britain in 1948 and 1954 to see if the level of productivity in an industry in a region was significantly associated with the size of the industry in the region.

3 AIMS OF THE STUDY

The aims of this study arise out of the findings of the four groups of earlier research studies listed above. The dominant general aim can be summarised as:-

(a) To examine whether the variations in productivity and efficiency by subregion within individual industrial sectors are statistically associated with variations in economic attributes of the subregions which reflect the availability of external economies for the operations of the sector.

Behind this general aim lie two subsidiary objectives:-

(b) To develop a set of variables which reflect the various possible elements of local external economies.

(c) To examine the spatial interrelationships between the various elements of local external economies.

Both the broad sweep of findings and the detailed consideration of fifty-three separate industrial sectors lead finally to a verdict on the importance of agglomeration economies for manufacturing industry in a highly developed industrialised nation such as the United Kingdom.

4 THE APPROACH USED

The research strategy for this study revolves around the central data set. The Business Statistics Office, at the request of the senior researcher, prepared a set of special tabulations from the raw data of the 1968 Census of Production. These tabulations provided for each product group in U.K. manufacturing industry a listing by region and subregion of net output per head, average number of employees per establishment, net output per establishment and wages and salaries as a percentage of net output. The strengths and weaknesses of this data are discussed in chapter five.

This data set provided three alternative measures of industrial efficiency by product group and by subregion (remembering that not every product group is represented in every subregion, and that disclosure problems also eliminated many potential observations). The three measures were net output per head, net output minus wages and salaries per head and a derived index of efficiency. The measures are described fully and evaluated in chapter four. The initial research task was to look for distinctive spatial patterns in these variables.

The central aim of the research, as suggested above, was to see if spatial variation in the efficiency measures were statistically associated with variables which reflected economies external to an industry in a subregion. A second data set was therefore built up of variables which reflected both economies of localisation (external to the firm but not the industry) and urbanisation economies (external to the industry). Because many of these variables are inexact measures of the concepts lying behind the different possible facets of economies of agglomeration, choices had to be made between alternative measures of the same concept. These choices were made on the basis of the spatial patterning of the variables and their intercorrelations. Key correlations between the agglomeration measures and the efficiency measures were also identified.

It was then possible to experiment with a number of regression models to link different subgroupings of the agglomeration variables to the efficiency measures. These regression models for a total of fifty-three product groups form the central core of the analytical results of this study.

The research strategy has been dominated by the fact that the Census of Production data comes from one year only. No analysis of changes in efficiency was therefore possible. Likewise, no information was available on capital or on investment. The analysis is perhaps rather narrowly based on the net output per head and associated measures. The researchers have been very much aware of this as a potential source of weakness. At the same time, the main data set provides a level of detail on net output by product group and by subregion which has never before been available to researchers in the United Kingdom. We have tried, with we hope appropriate caution, to exploit this data set to the full in order to gain a clearer perspective on whether the spatial context of industrial operations really is important to the efficiency and profitability of those operations.

5 AN OUTLINE OF THE CHAPTERS

Chapter two is an extension of sections one and two of this chapter. It discusses in some detail the concept of agglomeration economies, suggesting why they evolve and why their importance may be changing over time in the United Kingdom. The following chapter is complementary to this discussion. It sets out the empirical context of the present study, reviewing past research into the impact of agglomeration economies on the choice of locations by industrial companies; on the patterns of industrial movement involving the opening of new branch plants and the transfer of existing units to new sites; on the existence of local linkages; and on the spatial patterns of new investment. This research evidence comes primarily from the United Kingdom. There are some important differences in the findings between the two countries.

Chapter four introduces the variables used to measure the impact of different sources of agglomeration economy. The reasons for using three different dependent variables to reflect subregional differences in industrial efficiency are given. One of these variables is in the form of an index. Its derivation is provided. The data sources and quality are discussed. Nearly thirty variables were used to reflect different characteristics of the subregions which reflected the potential presence of different agglomeration economies. The reasons for choosing these and rejecting others are discussed in chapter five.

Presentation of the results of the analysis starts in chapter six. Here an outline and summary of the spatial variations across the sixty-one subregions is provided, together with differences between industrial sectors. The principal correlations between the dependent and independent variables are analysed in chapter seven by product group and by region. The problem of high levels of intercorrelation among some of the independent variables is first addressed here. The use of principal components analysis to reduce one of the largest groups of variables is explained at the end of this chapter.

Chapters eight and nine are the most important chapters, reflecting the analytical heart of the study. The particular forms of regression equation which were used are justified. A summary of the results is set out and interpreted. Particular attention is paid to the significance and signs of coefficients, rather than to the size of coefficients. Chapter ten provides a summary and discusses the implications of this study for future research.

2 Externalities and agglomeration economies

1 INTRODUCTION

In the past different meanings have been attached to the term 'agglomeration economies'. It has been a label for those external economies which arise from spatial proximity of industrial plants in the same and in different sectors and of related urban and industrial services. This is the usage followed here. The term has also been used to refer to the functional proximity of sectors of industrial activity in an input-output sense. Although the functional relationships may correspond to the local spatial linkages, they will also hold over much greater distances. The focus here remains at the local intra-urban and intra-subregional level.

Different meanings and usages suggest a need to define and illustrate the concept of economies of agglomeration. This is the task of this chapter. Following the development of the concept in the literature of economics, geography and regional science, the discussion here suggests why such economies are considered important and how theory would predict they would manifest themselves in practice.

2 THE CONCEPT OF AGGLOMERATION ECONOMIES

Agglomeration economies are a phenomenon of some considerable importance in urban and regional spatial analysis. They are thought to play a complex part in the spatial concentration of economic activity and their analysis and identification will throw some light on the reasons why economic activities in general and manufacturing establishments in particular are spread unevenly over space. Agglomeration economies might also help to explain why concentrations of manufacturing activity are of different sizes and of differing economic structures, and why the production of some industries is carried on in a few production units in a limited number of urban areas, while in other industries production is spread over a large number of plants in many different centres.

Richardson (1973) sees agglomeration economies as having four major inpacts:

(a) to boost the rate of technical progress and productivity.

(b) to attract industry or capital into a region or metropolitan area.

(c) to influence the decisions of households whether or not to migrate.

(d) to improve the efficiency of the urban regional spatial structure.

Since agglomeration economies have multiple roles, their benefits differ for different sections of society and it is therefore useful to draw a distinction between:

(a) Social Agglomeration Economies which include scale economies in urban services and the impact of urbanisation on both national growth and intra-regional efficiency. These economies affect all groups in society.

(b) Household Agglomeration Economies These refer to the benefits offered to the residents of large cities e.g wider variety of goods to purchase and services to enjoy, greater job opportunities.

(c) Business Agglomeration Economies These are the benefits enjoyed by business firms operating within cities. They are the major concern of this study.

Agglomeration economies occur when a firm can profit by locating in close proximity to other firms, or when it is profitable for one firm to grow very large by combining many different but associated processes in a single factory. The external economies accruing to industrial companies from an urban environment and from other companies include:

(a) Economies of a large labour market: the ability to choose in a large pool of varied skills, greater elasticity in labour supply, better training and educational facilities, the existence of recruiting and placement services, a larger supply of managerial and professional talent (and the consumption externalities to attract these).

(b) Opportunities for specialisation in products and processes, establighing local production linkages. This includes a pool of sub-contractors and technical production services.

(c) Transport cost savings in serving a local market and in access to transport and distribution services.

(d) Access to specialised business services in law, accountancy, insurance, banking, finance, and scientific advice; and to dealers in industrial materials and equipment, as well as to technical repairs and servicing.

(e) Economies of scale from the utilities such as water supply and other public services, in both cost and quality. (Although these externalities are more important in a developing nation than in a nation such as the U.K. where access to such services is fairly uniform across the country).

(f) Access to a large property market, and to secondhand equipment and specialist manufacturers and installers of capital goods, allowing adaptability and flexibility in fixed investment.

(g) More indefinable economies which arise from good communications and ease of face to face contact, encouraging innovation in products, in processes and in market development.

It is clear from this categorisation of agglomeration economies why the concept has become important in understanding the forces which lead to the concentration of manufacturing activity in space. There have been many attempts by locational theorists to explain in general why economic activity in most nations tends to be concentrated in comparatively few urban locations. Weber (1929), Hoover (1948) and Isard (1956) have all emphasised the relative importance of the group of economies which accrue to economic activities which cluster in space.

Weber (1929) provided one of the earliest theories to explain the location of manufacturing industry, suggesting three basic locational forces which influence the location of a firm under conditions of perfect competition. Within a cost minimisation framework, Weber developed a model to explain location on the basis of minimising transport costs, minimising labour costs and taking advantage of economies arising from agglomeration.

Weber defined an agglomerative factor as one which cheapened production when that production was concentrated at one place. Weber's agglomerative factors included economies of scale within a plant as well as economies which derive from the spatial association of several plants. He envisaged economies of association deriving from such items as the specialised division of labour between plants, the provision of better maintenance and repair facilities, specialised labour pools, the development of markets for both the materials and products of an industry and the lowering of social overhead costs. Within the Weberian analysis a plant would locate in an agglomeration if such savings offset any increased transport costs of material inputs or of the final products.

Weberian analysis is subject to numerous criticisms (Webber, 1972) not least of which is his perfect competition assumption. Lösch (1954) shows that minimum cost points of production are meaningless in imperfectly competitive systems with markets not distributed uniformly over space so that demand and hence price are variant upon location. Lösch therefore introduced the notion of markets through Central Place Theory, but the concept of agglomeration of selling points still remained significant in his analysis, with the selling points of different goods tending to cluster together to derive economies of agglomeration.

Agglomeration economies may result from both internal and external economies of scale, both of which may be consequent upon indivisibilities. Often agglomeration economies are seen as synonymous with external economies of scale alone, when used to explain the spatial concentration of manufacturing growth. Whilst most interest surrounds the purely external economies of scale, from a theoretical point of view both categories of scale economy can result in the emergence of agglomeration economies.

Bos (1965) argues that it is essential for a theory striving to explain the spatial dispersion of production to introduce the notion of indivisibility in commodities, factors of production, and the production processes. Indivisibilities do not allow proportionality to be maintained at all levels of production between all inputs in the production process and lead therefore to increasing returns to scale. This implies increasing output per unit of input or alternatively decreasing costs per unit of production. One result is the concentration of production in space. If this concentration occurs at the scale of the single firm or the single plant, then internal economies of scale are achieved. However if the effects of indivisibilities and scale are studied from the point of view of the industry or the economy, rather than from the point of view of the individual firm, external economies are achieved. For example, a firm may benefit from specialised financial services, or repair and maintenance services as a result of the general development of the economy or industry to which that firm belongs, because these operations only become profitable at some minimum level of production. External economies of scale can therefore result as a consequence of indivisibilities.

In sum therefore, agglomeration economies embrace both external and internal economies of scale. Internal economies are achieved as the production unit or plant increases in size. The optimum size will vary between activities and change with technological advances. These economies may be of a technical nature and occur in one location or they may be non-spatially orientated. Diseconomies of scale may begin to occur when a firm or plant has reached a certain size and with these diseconomies will come increasing unit costs of production. External economies may be either external to the firm and internal to the industry or external to both firm and industry.

3 CATEGORIES OF AGGLOMERATION ECONOMY

Hoover (1937) argued that economies of agglomeration, as Weber saw them, mixed three quite distinctly different forces affecting production costs. This distinction has subsequently been adopted universally by the literature. These forces are

(a) Large scale economies within a firm as a result of increases in the scale of production.

(b) Localisation economies for all firms in a single industry at a single location consequent upon the enlargement of the total output of that industry.

(c) Urbanisation economies for all firms and all industries at a single location consequent upon the enlargement of the total economic size of that location, for all industries taken together.

Each of these forces are today acknowledged as being of importance in the development and growth of metropolitan regions. To these we can add a separate category of diseconomies of agglomeration. Each will be considered in more detail.

(i) Internal economies of scale

In each industry, an optimum plant size or a minimum efficient plant size given by the lowest average unit cost of production, will normally exist with a given technology and set of input prices. This size or range of sizes depends on the interrelationship of four factors: technical, managerial, marketing and finance. Minimum average costs may not coincide for all factors at a given rate of production, although a large firm may be able to reduce average costs by the manner in which it combines the scale of operation of each factor. In multiplant companies certain functions may be centralised to serve more than one plant.

As plant size increases then economies of scale may be achieved, particularly as a result of specialisation and a division of labour. Large plants with large workforces permit narrow specialisation, increases in worker proficiency and less time loss when workers move between different production processes within the plant. Equally large scale production enables both extensive and intensive use of capital machinery, the introduction of more capital equipment leading to greater automation, the displacement of labour and a tendency to reduce the unit production costs.

Plant expansion beyond a certain point however can lead to diseconomies of scale. The introduction of multiple processes can lead to managerial problems, while at the shopfloor level worker alienation can set in as workers become more remote from the finished product.

(ii) Localisation economies

This term characterises advantages external to firms within a single industry. As the number of establishments in an industry increases in an area, localisation economies external to the industry are likely to develop. These include gravitation to sources of heavy raw materials or to non transportable factor inputs, the ability to support and have access to research and development facilities, and the development of common pools of highly specialised factors of production, which are shared by many firms in the industry.

In addition, as the industry develops in an area firms specialising in the repair and maintenance of machinery for that industry tend to become established, as do suppliers of materials and components for that industry. This allows firms to maintain smaller stocks and to develop a more efficient organisation of their principal inputs. Other economies of localisation include the development and access to specialised storage services, the acquisition of favourable freight rates at places of concentrated production, and the establishment of firms which specialise narrowly in the making of one or several intermediate inputs used by other firms in the industry. By concentrating in a single location firms specialising in these activities can develop internal economies of scale since they are able to operate on a scale large enough to serve many firms within one industry. Finally, intra-industry spatial concentration also results in a reduction in transport inputs associated with the import of factor inputs into an area or the distribution of final products from an area. Spatial concentration within an industry can however lead to diseconomies of scale through for example increased wage rates.

Richardson (1973) expresses the view that economies of localisation, although important, are not particularly relevant in explaining regional differentials in the strength of an agglomeration because they may be created anywhere depending on the availability of raw materials. The optimal agglomeration from the economies of localisation point of view will be determined by the trade off between external economies arising from the spatial links between firms in the industry and the internal economies of scale in production. This is simply because the external economies of scale will tend to increase as linkage increases while the internal economies will increase as the number of firms within the industry, and hence the number of local links between these firms, diminishes. Over time the distinction between localisation economies and internal economies of scale sometimes becomes blurred as large firms internalise those very processes which smaller firms within that industry had previously provided. Alternatively, large firms may reach a particular size when they choose to go outside for certain specific needs, and it is for this reason economies of localisation are more likely to influence the location of small firms. In particular, new small firms, lacking capital, may be especially dependent upon localisation economies in the first few years of their existence. Some of these firms will only be able to survive in locations where these externalities are present.

(iii) Urbanisation economies

These are closely related to economies of localisation but tend to vary with city size. Urbanisation economies offer advantages to firms in all industries as a result of the total economic size of an urban agglomeration (population, income, output, and wealth). Thus urbanisation economies represent for all firms and all industries the savings from the large scale operation of the agglomeration as a whole. For any given company or production unit, the economies of urbanisation will normally include: access to a large labour force offering a variety of skills and talent; the local avilability of capital; the presence of wholesaling facilities allowing a reduction in the stock levels which need to be held; high levels of efficiency and quality in public services; the presence of local supply industries; and the market potential which arises from the spatial concentration of population, industry and income. Urbanisation economies also include the presence of specialised business services such as financial and banking services, and local business consultancy and ancillary services (advertising, legal, computing, R. and D.). Interindustry juxtaposition also allows a reduction in transport inputs required to bring inputs to and take output from the production plant. The relative concentration of higher order facilities such as universities, polytechnics, offices of central government, exhibition centres, conference halls, hotels, theatres and concert halls, can provide indirect economies to production activities.

The nature of these agglomeration economies is therefore seen to be extremely varied. The existence of even a few of these economies can mean that new firms find the process of becoming established simpler than they might have done otherwise, or that established firms can operate more efficiently. In densely concentrated industrial areas for example there tends to be a greater availability of factory premises which means that entrepreneurs wishing to set up in business or those firms needing to expand the scale of their operations can usually find premises close to their homes or existing sites. For new entrepreneurs the pool of cheap secondhand premises may be crucially important.

The growth of urbanisation economies with city size is likely to increase as the range of economic and social functions operating within the agglomeration increases, and as the population increases. While the exact structure of these functions will vary between cities of a given size, the general range will be similar. However, the cumulative advantage to industrial firms locating in larger and larger metropolitan areas is eventually offset by countervailing forces.

(iv) Diseconomies of agglomeration

A major problem for any theory of regional development that emphasises economies of agglomeration is to explain why people and industry do not crowd together in just one location in a national economy. The existence of diseconomies of agglomeration must also be recognised. Isard (1956) attempted to investigate the notion of the optimal scale of agglomeration using the concept of net economy (economies less diseconomies) for a combination of net economy curves for agglomerations of varying size. Each net economy curve represented a different aspect of the economy, curves summing to give a economy curve. Theoretically at least it should be possible to draw household curves and industry curves. Since people and industries cluster into urban centres of different sizes to achieve their own best balance between agglomeration benefits, urban services, and transport costs, these curves would have different profiles as would disaggregations within the industry and household groups. Thus net diseconomies for firms will arise at different sizes of agglomeration than diseconomies for households. Many of the external costs of production are borne by the community (such as increased congestion, pollution, noise, longer journey to work trips) and thus households may begin to incur diseconomies of agglomeration before net agglomeration economies become negative for the industries in the same urban area.

Although large and varied urban areas are presumed to confer the greatest net advantages of agglomeration, excessive concentration in these areas can lead to a reduction of local interdependence between firms and industries, for two reasons. As agglomerations grow in physical size, the boundaries of the area are pushed out and firms within any one agglomeration are increasingly separated geographically. This can lead to reductions in contact between firms especially on a face to face basis, or to increasing costs of communication and transportation should the firms wish to engage in frequent contact. Equally if the boundaries of the agglomeration remain fixed, growth must imply increased concentration which may spell congestion, frustrating communication, as well as adding time costs to the movement of goods.

From a theoretical standpoint the optimal size of an agglomeration for industry is reached when a single extra factory harms those already established by the diseconomies that it causes to exactly the same extent as it provides benefits (in terms of enlarging the labour market, encouraging common services, cheapening supplies of components and producing other external economies of scale). The optimal size for any agglomeration will depend on the types of firms and industries that make up that agglomeration, and on the trade offs with the costs and benefits to households.

Examples of general diseconomies of agglomeration for firms are congestion, pollution, higher land costs, higher cost of premises, higher labour costs, the age of the premises, and the congestion of premises which prevent factory extension. These all affect the cost and efficiency of manufacturing. Once again, we can distinguish diseconomies of scale internal to the firm from those external to the firm but internal to the industry and from those external to the industry. Overall, these diseconomies may be seen as one set of reasons why movement away from the central urban areas has occurred in recent years in many developed countries, leading to the growth of the metropolitan suburbs and of free standing towns, away from the main metropolitan area. (Vining and Kontuly, 1978).

4 STATIC AND DYNAMIC INTERDEPENDENCE

Economies of localisation and urbanisation mean that sites in large urban areas can offer clear economic advantages to many firms. The way in which these advantages are conferred upon different firms and industries can be explored with the aid of two related concepts: one static, the other dynamic. The static concept is based on competitive equilibrium theory and sees economies arising when input prices fall for the plant demanding those inputs for reasons outside of its control. As such the full social costs of that plant's production are never reflected in the output price because of a divergence between the social and the private costs. This concept serves to aid the understanding of economies arising from direct linkage between firms. The dynamic concept arises from an interdependence between firms in investment and changes in output, and includes the static concept of economies of scale, as well as embracing the idea that spillover effects of investment by one firm are unplanned in terms of their effects on related firms.

Firms operating within an agglomeration may find themselves in a situation where they have little choice but to benefit from or suffer the consequences of evolving opportunities. There are many different paths of interdependence which pose considerable problems of empirical identification and evaluation. Sveikhauskas (1975), while recognising the significance of the static concept in suggesting increased specialisation and division of labour leading to increases in productivity, argues that the more important productivity advantages are the dynamic benefits of urban concentration. Cities are the centres of activity where business is concentrated and where the new ideas and the new innovations that are at the heart of technological progress are likely to occur. Pred (1966), and Jacobs (1970) have also stressed this dynamic advantage of cities for economic activity. Technological progress improves the productivity of both capital and labour.

5 THE EVOLUTION OF AGGLOMERATION ECONOMIES

The notion of linkages between plants, between firms, and between industries is fundamental to the understanding of agglomeration economies of localisation and urbanisation. These external economies are reflected in the existence of local industrial linkages.

The term linkage relates to links between firms or establishments that are necessary for those establishments to operate, or that enhance the efficiency of the full production process. Early definitions of linkage concentrated upon the identification of links by direction of sales; forward, backward, diagonal, vertical, horizontal, lateral (Florence 1948). Wood (1969) has argued for a concept of industrial linkage which embraces the flow of information between establishments as well as goods. In the final analysis any firm is but one part of a complex chain of production held together by direct or indirect linkages. While linkages can exist over very great distances, perhaps between different nations, in many sectors of industry goods linkages occur with greatest intensity within localised areas where manufacturing processes are closely interrelated e.g. in the West Midlands conurbation.

A different form of industrial linkage associated with economies of scale but not at one point in space, is that of organisation and control within multiplant firms. Pred(1975) discusses the significance of non local multiplant linkages between metropolitan complexes and the overall pattern of metropolitan interdependence that arises from the spatial structure of these multiplant organisations. There are virtually always important decision making, information flow and service provision linkages connecting an organisation's headquarters and its subservient units whether spatially proximate or distant.

It is through linkages that external economies as defined are transmitted to individual production units and sectors of industry. Lloyd and Dicken (1977) define three types of linkage:-

(a) Production Linkage. This involves the physical movement of goods within the chain of production. These linkages tend to be more important for smaller businesses which often become specialised linked elements in a production chain. Larger firms are often able to internalise their links with their own production process.

(b) Service Linkages. These connect a producer to services ancillary to the production process itself. This group will include links to suppliers of machinery and equipment etc., and also to suppliers of professional services such as accountants, solicitors, and to other services such as window cleaners, repair facilities, providers of stationery, etc.

(c) Marketing Linkages. These tie the commercial sector involved in selling and distribution to the products of a particular producer. The sector includes wholesalers, packagers, transport firms, sales agencies and advertising agencies.

As demonstrated by the Lloyd and Dicken classification, linkage between firms occurs at most stages of industrial development. As the economy evolves however two different processes tend to influence the structure of manufacturing industry. Firstly as technology advances, and company ownership and organisation develop, there is a tendency for the smaller firms and units to be absorbed into large units which give economies of scale in production and distribution. The development of the large corporation becomes necessary to carry out research into new products and methods of production, to finance their introduction, and to internalise service, market and production linkages within a single organisation in order to maintain control throughout the whole production process. Thus there is an integration process over time. However, at the same time a process of differentiation and specialisation can also be observed. Hoover (1948, p. 120) points to particular scale economies which come from the specialisation of functions:

'Certain operations and services that a firm in a smaller place would do for itself can in the city be farmed out to separate enterprises specialising in these operations and operating at a scale large enough to do the job more cheaply.'

Thus economies of scale from serving a large urban market are seen to make the small specialist enterprise cost efficient. These internal economies to the specialist are then passed on through to other firms that use the specialist's goods and services. The process of disintegration as a consequence of operating within a large market is perhaps less common today since large firms with extensive funds often have a strong desire to diversify to spread risk, and will use internal services in order to guarantee supply and to control quality.

Fragmentation will still occur however where specialist knowledge seeks a personal financial reward outside the framework of a large corporation. Thus disintegration can result from a change in technology, where the technology is pioneered by small firms hoping to exploit the market for their own ends. The birth process of new independent firms therefore tends to be concentrated in sectors where skill and innovation are rewarded most quickly and where a large capital investment is not a necessary requirement. In addition, the externally linked firms will often operate in sectors where both technology and the forces of demand are changing rapidly. They therefore rely on small firms to serve their changing needs. Thus small firms operate in high risk sectors and are likely to experience high birth rates and high death rates as the sector evolves.

The logic of inter-firm linkages of this kind, and hence economies of localisation and urbanisation, stems from specialisation. Given sufficient demand, specialisation can prove economic and reduce costs at no loss of product or service quality. Successful specialisation depends upon the minimisation of total costs and therefore, all else being equal, economies from industrial linkage are likely to be at their greatest when the distance between supplier and customer is at a minimum. Within concentrations or clusters of economic activity, the importance of agglomeration economies depends in part upon the rapidity with which communication between customer and supplier can take place. Townroe (1970) suggested that face to face contact played a critical role for small firms in their early life, when the need to be rapidly responsive to opportunities is crucial. The immediacy of communication has particular importance to firms making non standard items, offering one off serivces. Commercial printing, lithography, women's apparel and certain elements of the electronics industry are good examples. Brown (1972) suggested that the need for face to face contact, together with the growth of specialists in both the manufacturing and service sector to serve the large integrated firms, are factors which are likely to maintain the importance of agglomeration economies today.

Linkage then, tends to be found more strongly between processes that are specialised by skill, and which produce and use non uniform and custom built goods. These processes have to be adaptable and sensitive to technical change. Quickly established and quickly broken local linkages serve the interests of many larger firms as well as allowing new small enterprises to become established. The significance of economies of agglomeration may diminish in the future with an increasing proportion of large firms in the economy able to internalise their own services, train their own staff and produce standardised products through automated processes without the need for specialists. Against this, certain categories of service seem to be increasing, even for large companies. Wage packeting and payment, hiring and leasing, factoring, and computer services are all examples of increasing services. The rapid development of telecommunications, computer links, and the modern transport network have also tended to speed up the circulation of both information and products, and inevitably therefore have tended to reduce the advantages associated with clustering of economic activity in space. It can equally be argued however that the general improvement in communications of all types has increased the spatial area over which economies of agglomeration can now be achieved. McCrone (1969) suggests that for many types of industry an area as large as South Wales or Central Scotland is not too large to give rise to external economies of scale.

3 Evidence for the importance of agglomeration economies

The empirical studies which yield evidence as to the role and significance of agglomeration economies come from a variety of backgrounds. This chapter reviews three groups of British and American studies which have placed agglomeration economies as one factor among several in:

(a) explaining both the pressures behind transfer moves of industrial establishments and the opening of new branch plants and the factors attracting this mobile investment to a new location;

(b) understanding the causes of differences between areas of relative rates of industrial growth and decline; and

(c) considering spatial variations in labour productivity.

This study has evolved from the last of these three groups of studies but key hypotheses do emerge from the findings of all three groups. The chapter also briefly reviews studies of local economic linkages between industrial plants and studies which attempt to relate spatial clustering of different industrial sectors to their functional interdependence.

1 AGGLOMERATION ECONOMIES AND LOCATIONAL CHOICE

Many location decisions in the eighteenth and nineteenth centuries were based on raw material supply considerations, and urban centres tended to develop around the sources of raw materials. Today many of the original advantages associated with these locations have ceased to exist. However, historical inertia and well established local linkages between industrial plants have tended to maintain the original spatial patterns. From these origins significant decentralisation trends can now be identified in the location of new firms and in the establishment of branch plants and the transfer of existing industrial units to new sites. These trends are reviewed in this section with a view to identifying the significance of agglomeration economies in influencing location choice. As Richardson (1973, p. 99) suggests:

> 'To the extent that regions grow because their urban centres grow, and to the extent that regional growth is associated with changes in the distribution of population that favour metropolitan areas, then agglomeration economies may be a critical variable in the migration function.'

i) Movement patterns

(a) Intra-urban movement A trend towards a reduction in employment density in city centres, and a fall in the employment density centre to periphery, has been identified in a number of major cities in both the United States and the United Kingdom. Creamer (1963), Mills (1972), Harrison(1974)(1), Kain (1975)(2) have all produced evidence of a process of decentralisation in the United States. In the United Kingdom planning controls, especially in relation to agricultural land constraints and green belts, have tended to limit the strength of decentralisation. However, Bull (1978), Gripaios (1977) and Keeble (1968) have shown empirically that decentralisation has been taking place in London and Glasgow. Lever (1975) has produced evidence for Glasgow and Birmingham. Bull and Gripaios found that suburban growth of manufacturing employment at the expense of city centre growth was more the result of suburban plant birth and city centre deaths than net out migration. Keeble however found considerable evidence of actual out migration from London in the form of both branch plants and complete transfers.

(b) Intra-regional movement In the U.S. and U.K. industrial migration beyond the metropolitan suburbs to free standing towns and villages has also been a phenomenon since the 1950's. 'Counter-urbanisation' (Berry and Gillard, 1977) has been taking place in the U.S. and the evidence suggests that the decentralisation process is job led. Haren (1970) showed that between 1962 and 1969 the largest labour markets in the U.S. were gaining new jobs relatively more slowly than the remainder so that by 1969 the large labour markets accounted for 71% of all manufacturing jobs but only 67% of new manufacturing jobs. From 1970-74 the trend continued with non metropolitan areas experiencing manufacturing employment growth of 13.9% compared to the metropolitan areas' 3.0%. In the U.K. evidence of manufacturing growth is less clear cut. However, the outer metropolitan areas experienced accelerated population and employment growth 1961-71 compared with the previous decade (Townroe, 1979). Keeble (1976) demonstrates the dispersal of manufacturing jobs in the South East region between 1966 and 1971 with growth going to small towns and rural areas of Kent, Sussex, Hampshire and areas north of London.

(c) Inter-regional movement Industrial movements between regions in both the United States and the United Kingdom have been common since the 1950's. In the U.S. it has been characterised by the growth of the sun belt states and west coast states, while in the U.K., East Anglia and the South West experienced the highest percentage growth rates in both population and employment terms between 1961-75, and significant industrial movement was induced by the Assisted Area policy.

Overall in both the U.S. and the U.K. four main trends present themselves: the process of decentralisation of manufacturing industry and employment from the historically significant metropolitan core areas; the accompanying growth of the metropolitan suburbs; growth in other parts of the region outside of the metropolitan area; and the inter-regional industrial migration towards the less urban regions and policy influenced movement to the Assisted Areas.

(ii) Agglomeration economies and reasons for decentralisation

Decentralisation from the metropolitan core could result either from the birth of firms outside of the area and deaths within it, or from migration away from the area. The process of the birth of firms outside of the central city area is considered with the choice of location by migrant firms in the next section. While the deaths of metropolitan manufacturing firms can result from a change in the nature of, or loss of economies of agglomeration, these pressures also act as a spur to out migration. Out migration is the main concern of this section.

The traditional economies of spatial propinquity associated with city centre locations are perhaps less binding today than in the past. Suburban locations offer pools of labour previously associated with city centre locations. Equally traditional urban services have become more diffused throughout whole metropolitan areas. And large firms have internalised many of their services and hence rely upon their own organisation. For example, Britton (1974) showed in a survey in Ontario how the key auditing, legal and financial services were usually procured from non Ontario metropolitan complexes because in most cases each plant was part of a multilocational organisation. Interfirm linkages are less and less local. For example, Lever (1974) showed that about 80% of 1970 purchases made by twenty-four glass, electrical machinery, paper, tool, paint and clothing factories in Glasgow involved centres outside of Scotland. This reliance on non Scottish suppliers reflects the multilocational structure of organisations in manufacturing industry in Scotland and a nationwide or international focus in purchasing. Headquarters are often located in London and supply procurement decisions are frequently a central responsibility. Pred (1976) reviews numerous examples of non local industrial linkages from many studies.

Improved systems and methods of communication also reduce the significance of distance within cities for all types of industry. Thus plants are less tied to city centre locations than in the past and linkage is less distance dependent. Keeble (1976) attributes the increased distance over which firms relocate in the South East to the improvement of radial communications (amongst other factors), because this enables them to maintain their ties with the capital. Keeble (1969) equally explains the radial migration preference for locations to the west and north west of London by firms previously located in North West London, by their desire for easy contact with specialists in the area from which the firms originated. This easy contact was facilitated by the first class roads and motorways radiating from the area of origin. McCarthy and Morrison (1978) have also concluded that increases in accessibility have increased the distances over which links can now be maintained whilst also suggesting that economies of agglomeration are less significant today in the United States.

In addition Struyk and James (1975) found little evidence of Hoover and Vernon's original incubator hypothesis, which emphasised the importance of high density central locations within cities for small manufacturing establishments, resulting from the advantage of external economies through linkage. Struyk and James found that new manufacturing establishments were not disproportionately core concentrated in Boston, Cleveland, Minneapolis, St. Paul and Phoenix. For many industries, the balance of advantage has been changing. Segal (1960) showed that the importance of links in those sectors traditionally highly dependent upon local linkage was lessening in New York in the 1950's. For example, industries producing ledgers, sales forms, printing, book binding moved away from the centre to lower wage areas, but within relatively easy driving time of the metropolitan area.

As well as a change in the nature of agglomeration economies, movement away from city centre locations by manufacturing establishments might reflect the growing significance of diseconomies of agglomeration. Social factors such as rising crime, increased congestion and pollution and strict land controls may act as push factors in the process of decentralisation. Other phenomena arising from a concentration of economic activity are of course high prices for both land and premises and lack of space to expand. Keeble (1976) points to external diseconomies in larger cities as one reason for the changing trend towards longer distance migration of firms in the South East 1966-74.

The I.L.A.G. (3) survey 1973-74 throws some light on the significance of diseconomies for the movement of firms in the U.K. between 1964 and 1967. From a response of 543 firms (69%) the three most common reasons for opening a new manufacturing plant in a new location are set out below. (Source: I.L.A.G. Survey, p. 523).

Table 3.1

Reasons why firms considered opening a new plant in a new location	Percentage of all respondent firms		
	Major reason	Minor reason	Outstanding single reason
To permit an expansion of output	83	8	20
Inadequate existing premises or site	50	11	8
Unsatisfactory labour supply at existing location (1)	40	11	15

(1) This reflects the inability of firms to pay sufficiently high wages to draw sufficient labour to the site.

Inadequate premises often because of plans to expand, were therefore an important push factor. This factor was a more important reason for firms in Greater London and the South East region than for firms originally based elsewhere, and for small plant firms and firms in the metal manufacturing, timber, and other manufacturing industries. However, in certain industries, notably food, drink and tobacco, clothing, footwear, bricks, pottery, glass and cement, this factor was much less important. The survey also revealed that material and service linkage problems were a very minor reason for opening a new plant in a new location. Only 3% of firms considered their distance from raw materials, components and industrial and commercial services as a major reason for relocation.

Similar results for Boston come from Hamer (1973) in a survey of 222 firms in 1969. Proximity to customers and suppliers was given as a reason for not considering a move by 13% and 32% respectively. This however is in contrast to Economic Consultants Ltd. (1971) who recorded that 'access to buyers of your product and service' was felt to be important and essential by more than 50% of firms surveyed, while access to suppliers of goods and materials was felt to be essential by 29% of firms surveyed (although the term 'access' was not tightly defined).

Keeble (1969) found that decentralisation was not impeded by local linkages. Movement out of North West London, especially by metal fabricating and engineering firms was brought about mainly by a wish to expand production and tended to be most common amongst those larger firms not tied by technology and organisation to specific locations.

Firms with a high level of dependence upon labour and land have frequently been forced to move away from central locations, as Lever (1975) records in a study of Glasgow and Birmingham. Firms with a low dependence, despite rising costs have been able to maintain central locations. Thus firms drawn to city centres by the presence of external economies where possible substitute a new set of spatial characteristics into their production functions as a result of rising input costs. In contrast, Cameron and Johnson (1969) show that of thirty-nine firms in Glasgow forced to relocate through redevelopment, thirty-seven chose to stay close to the city centre largely for reasons of access to the labour market. However, only four of the thirty-nine firms employed more than one hundred people.

As far as it is possible to explain the decentralisation process through agglomeration economies it seems that it has been in part in response to a reduction in the significance of some agglomeration economies as well as to a broadening of the area over which economies of agglomeration can be achieved, and to the existence of certain diseconomies in the face of plans to expand production.

(iii) Agglomeration economies and the choice of location

The significance of agglomeration economies for locational choice differs with the source of agglomeration economies; the distance over which the move takes place; and the type of industry, the nature of the firm (branch or transfer) and its size.

(a) Sources of agglomeration economies In the Struyk and James (1975) study of intra-metropolitan industrial migration within Cleveland, Minneapolis - St. Paul, Boston and Phoenix, the influence of births and deaths more than outweighed migration effects in explaining employment growth outside of the city centre. Within central locations they demonstrate that spatial concentrations of industry are important in influencing location and employment growth and suggest that for a limited number of concentrated industries, notably apparel and printing and publishing, external economies are the most important influence on locational behaviour.

In a comparison of Birmingham and Glasgow, Lever (1975) showed that in Birmingham, with a high coefficient of specialisation (and hence the probability of a group of industries enjoying a market comparative advantage and experiencing external economies through local linkage), between 1959 and 1969 manufacturing plants had a death rate of 2.7% per annum, a birth rate of 2.52% and a mover rate of 2.56%. This compared with 2.77% per annum, 2.09% and 2.86% in Glasgow where the index of specialisation was low. Thus specialisation seems largely to be inversely related to movement, as a theory of agglomeration economies would suggest. In Birmingham with a high dependence upon external economies, the birth rate of new manufacturing plants was higher by 20%, and the movement rate was lower by 11%, than experienced in Glasgow. These two conurbations were chosen by Lever because the industrial structure of Glasgow is most typical of the United Kingdom average, while that of Birmingham is the most dissimilar.

In the United States again Stone (1974) shows that external economies are important in explaining cross movement within Boston, in spite of the overall pattern of industrial migration away from the central location. He emphasises the importance of skilled labour pools for migrant industry. Schmenner (1978) in his study of Cincinnati also suggests the importance of local linkage given the high percentage of short distance moves between 1971 and 1975. Over 70% were moves of less than six miles and up to 90% were classed as local.

James and Hughes (1973), Keeble (1968) and Sant (1975) show in their analyses of intra-regional movement in the United States and United Kingdom that small firms were more reluctant to migrate away from the metropolitan zone than large firms. Keeble, for example, found that 66% of moves of over ten miles from North West London were by firms employing over one hundred employees while this group of firms only accounted for 38% of all firms in the sample. If, as theory would suggest, external economies are more important to small firms, then the patterns of movement should suggest that agglomeration economies do influence the location decisions of smaller firms. Keeble's work certainly seems to endorse this view. Smaller firms in his study tended to move within fifteen to twenty miles radius of London. Mechanical engineering and timber firms in particular fell within the group which needed to keep in close contact with the London market, and desired frequent and personal contact and the provision of rapid on the spot services.

The I.L.A.G. survey shows the importance of certain individual factors reflecting external economies in influencing locational decisions:

(i) Labour supply As we have seen an inadequate labour supply was a major reason affecting the decision to move. Besides acting as a push factor, particularly for smaller firms, labour supply considerations were found to be very significant in locational choice. It was a major factor for 72% of all firms, and the outstanding single factor for 20% of all firms. (Respondents could quote more than one 'major' factor.) It was less important for short distance movers, only 52% considering it a major factor in moves of less than twenty miles. Compared with branch plant moves, transfers also tended to consider it slightly less important, 64% classifying the factor as major. In contrast, 88% of long distance movers (over 250 miles) considered labour supply a major factor. A large labour pool is clearly one agglomeration economy which exercises a major influence on locational choice.

(ii) Managerial and staffing ties to an earlier location This factor was considered to be a major determinant of location for 24% of all cases. As might be expected the role played by this factor declined significantly with distance moved. Over moves less than twenty miles, 63% of the group felt these links to be of major importance, but only 22% for moves of 100-149 miles.

(iii) Supplies of raw materials and components Just as this factor was of little significance in prompting relocation so it was only a major factor for 15% of all cases in influencing location. For those firms that did take this factor into account raw materials were a more frequent consideration than were components.

(iv) Industrial and commercial services This factor was not at all influential in locational choice overall, but for the 3% of firms which considered it a major determinant the incidence of this supply factor fell away rapidly with distance moved.

(v) Access to markets This factor was considered to be a major factor for 30% of all firms in making a decision to relocate. 11% of all firms felt access to existing home markets was a major reason for not moving too far away, whilse 27% were moving to gain access to markets. The influence of this factor did not show any regular change with the distance over which the move took place. The highest figure was 47% for firms moving within 100 and 149 miles. The influence of this factor varied widely however with industry group and with the labour intensity of the industry. For example, for the building material (69%), paper and printing (58%), and food and drink (50%) sectors this factor was important; much less so for the clothing, footwear, mechanical and electrical engineering sectors. 46% of capital intensive firms considered markets a major factor, compared to 21% of labour intensive firms. Although 'access' as such need not necessarily imply spatial propinquity, these results suggest that for many firms access to markets is one source of agglomeration economy.

(b) Distance moved and location Since economies of agglomeration are primarily to be found in local linkages one would expect *a priori* that agglomeration advantages would be less important for long distance movers which would not necessarily be seeking new agglomeration economies. Keeble (1968) showed that the presence of important local linkages tended to be associated with short distance moves and smaller firms. Larger firms tended to open branch plants in more distant parts, attracted by large labour pools. This was confirmed in the I.L.A.G. Survey. Intre-regional moves were mainly in response to a clear push, whereas inter-regional moves tended to result more from choice and a decision to expand output. The former tended to be transfer moves, the latter branch moves. Although labour supply considerations were important to all movers, its relative importance increased for longer distance movers. In Assisted Areas government inducements and labour availability were critical influencing factors; four out of five firms selecting Assisted Area locations regarded labour availability as a major determining factor. In the non Assisted Areas and outside the New and Expanding Towns, labour supply was again an outstanding factor, but access to markets and suppliers ranked next in importance.

2 AGGLOMERATION ECONOMIES AND INDUSTRIAL GROWTH

There is a very extensive range of theoretical and empirical literature on manufacturing location dynamics. Approaches to the analysis of manufacturing growth and its spatial and regional variations, when measured by employment, value added, or other measures can conveniently be seen in terms of alternative conceptual models (Keeble, 1976). The first, the centre-periphery model, explains growth in terms of forces encouraging cumulative manufacturing growth in the main industrial core regions of the country at the expense of the more isolated peripheral areas. The second model explains growth occurring away from the main industrial centres as a consequence of centrifugal forces acting to disperse manufacturing growth.

The first of these models, the centre-periphery model, explains the growth of the dominant, centrally located and most prosperous regions, through six key factors: market accessibility, innovation leadership, quality of transport facilities, agglomeration economies, labour supply advantages, and entrepreneurial and institutional factors, where agglomeration economies are defined in their narrowest sense as resulting from inter-firm linkages. The spatial propinquity of all the above characteristics can provide economies for a firm located in a metropolitan area and can therefore be viewed as reasons why agglomerations provide external economies of production.

The periphery-centre model postulates industrial growth away from the main centre as being encouraged by labour supply advantages, agglomeration diseconomies, physical resource access, and government regional policy.

(i) Evidence from the United States

The impact of the processes inherent in both periphery-centre and centre-periphery models have received considerable attention from studies both in the United States and United Kingdom. Two research exercises in the United States by Burrows, Metcalf and Kaler (1971) and by Harris and Hopkins (1972) suggested that agglomeration effects were important in influencing industrial regional and subregional growth in the time periods considered.

The Burrows-Metcalf-Kaler study developed a model or set of models for 3,097 counties in the United States to forecast their future industrial structures on the basis of a limited number of easily obtainable socio-economic variables. The final model was designed to obtain ten year projections of employment by industry for every county in the United States, giving expected 1970 employment from 1960 socio-economic data. In both discriminant and regression equations, but more especially in the latter, the rate of population growth was found to have a very strong impact upon location. This variable was important for both manufacturing and service industries. Thus those counties with a high growth of population in the past were found likely to exhibit a high growth in the future. The authors were cautious about deriving cause and effect relationships, but they did find, using a variable of distance to the nearest S.M.S.A., that external economies of scale appeared to be present for firms locating near to medium sized centres (over 250,000 population) but as city size increased to over one million, the external economies failed to increase further.

Harris and Hopkins (1972) introduced a number of proxy variables into their inter-regional, multi-industry disequilibrium model to reflect economies from agglomeration. Their model was designed to examine the effect of regional factor prices and agglomeration on the location of manufacturing, using regression analysis. Using the concept of inertia (from the centre-periphery model) the model defines agglomeration factors as those that operate to keep firms in a region longer than relative factor prices themselves would suggest likely e.g. a highly skilled labour force or a well developed regional infrastructure.

The model is based on the assumption that firms locate in order to maximise profits and that 'in their locational decisions, firms examine the differences in regional product prices, input prices, and externalities; therefore regional changes in an industry's output should be responsive to these factors.' (p. 14).

Location equations were developed for eighty-four industrial sectors, the dependent variable being change in net output between 1965 and 1966. The marginal costs of obtaining inputs, transporting output and measures of agglomeration effects (4) were used as explanatory variables. Because of the lack of information on the marginal costs associated with externalities, agglomeration variables were included in the model to capture the effect of externalities on change in output.

The variables used to represent agglomeration effects were:

1 Population density

2 Output of major supplying industry

3 Purchases of major buyers of output by industry

4 Level of an industry's prior output level

5 Level of industries' capital stock.

The model was successful in explaining much of the variance in the change in output by county for most industries. Harris and Hopkins were concerned to use the data available to achieve a good specification of the location equations in order to get a meaningful model with coefficients that could be explained theoretically, rather than trying to maximise R^2. Specification of the model was achieved by ordering the variables according to hvpothesised theoretical importance. Agglomeration variables were entered last. All the eighteen variables played some part in the estimated equations although different variables were significant for different industries. The first three of the five agglomeration variables were significant for a large minority of sectors.

The study found transportation variables to be of particular importance, one being significant for sixty-one of the eighty-four industries studied. Although not considered by Harris and Hopkins as an economy of agglomeration, transportation cost savings will result from spatial propinquity with suppliers and markets and in their more general sense can be seen as an economy of agglomeration.

Two other United States studies by Richardson (1974) and Wheat (1973) have been less successful in explaining industrial growth variations through agglomeration effects. Wheat used data from the forty-eight contiguous states in the United States to measure regional growth patterns and regional influences. Three dependent variables (absolute, per capita and percentage growth in manufacturing employment) were correlated for years 1947-1963 with measures of the influence of markets, labour resources, agglomeration effects, climate, threshold size and urban orientation. The study drew upon thirteen basic variables which were extended with variations (roots, ratios, etc.) to reflect the hypothesised causal influences of growth.

The findings of this study showed that markets and climate were the leading influences affecting manufacturing growth in the United States. Labour and threshold size were found to be secondary influences, and resource and urban attraction of lesser importance. Agglomeration was found to have no measurable effect. Wheat's writing off of agglomeration seems however to be rather premature since certain advantages of industrial agglomeration could be the principal factors behind the threshold influence and the urban attraction. In addition the market factors and labour factors may also conceal certain agglomeration influences (for example intermediate markets have been counted as market factors, supplier firms selling to labour orientated industry have been counted as labour influences). The state scale of analysis is also rather coarse to pick up agglomeration effects.

Nevertheless Wheat's conclusions cannot be totally discounted and Richardson (1974) in his study of the determinants of growth in the United States between 1955 and 1964, was hardly more successful in defining a significant and strong relationship between growth and agglomeration economics. His study reported on the determinants of regional growth at the state level using gross state product estimates to measure growth and twenty-eight independent variables. These were broken down into groups representing testable hypotheses relating to demographic, amenity, agglomeration, business behaviour, labour market and policy variables.

The variables used to test the agglomeration hypotheses were: population; population density; scientific and technical personnel; regional growth; national urban hierarchy rank; employment growth in central administrative offices; telephone calls; income density; migration attraction; and income potential. The relationship between these factors and state product growth was tested using regression analysis, with very poor results. Only migration attraction and communication economies (measured by telephone calls) performed at all well. Richardson however derived a best fit equation using step wise regression on all twenty-eight variables without constraints imposed by preconceived hypotheses. This suggested that agglomeration factors were not totally redundant in explaining variations in state growth rates. Population, income density, locational preference and migration attraction, all representing the spatial distribution of population and economic activity, were associated with growth.

(ii) Evidence from the United Kingdom

In the United States the influence of agglomeration economies in industrial growth is not conclusive. Likewise, in the United Kingdom recent and current shifts in the spatial distribution of manufacturing industry has been accompanied by a controversy over the causes of regional variations in manufacturing growth rates. The structural school of thought argues that slow industrial growth in the peripheral regions stems from over specialisation in industries where demand has been either static or falling. The locational school accept this historical legacy, but stress the lack of access to markets and to suppliers in the poor growth performance of peripheral regions, since the modern growth industries have been attracted to central locations such as the South East and the Midlands. Implicit in the locational argument is the view that agglomeration linkages are important and that regional policy aimed at steering industry to low growth regions will have limited effect.

Chisholm and Oeppen (1973) studied the influence of industrial growth on the spatial distribution of employment between 1959 and 1968 over sixty-one British subregions at the Minimum List Heading level, looking at the relationship between growth and trends in diversification and specialisation. They show that the relationship between location and manufacturing structure weakened substantially over the period. Between 1959 and 1968 there was an average trend towards the diversification of subregional industrial structures and a strong trend towards the employment structure of each region converging towards a national average. Diversification tended to be more pronounced in the peripheral subregions (in part, because of regional policy). There was also a complementary trend for industries to be less localised particularly in manufacturing. These trends perhaps suggest that agglomeration economies are becoming less significant as industry becomes more dispersed and the employment structure more diversified.

Although subregions each have a different mix of industries, Chisholm and Oeppen found that industries either in decline or in expansion tended to be the same across all subregions despite the many processes of diversification and specialisation occurring between 1959 and 1968. They therefore tested to see if the structures of some subregions induced a worse growth performance than others. The traditionally worst off areas (Assisted Areas) were found to have significantly no more declining industries and no more growth industries than other areas. This suggested therefore that their poor performance in employment growth/unemployment terms reflects more the collective performance of minor industries rather than the major declining and expanding sectors. The authors suggested that this finding emphasised the importance of inter-industry linkages at the local level. The success of regional policy in the late sixties has however modified these trends by the early seventies.

A number of other studies have looked more specifically at the importance of agglomeration economies for employment growth in the United Kingdom. For example, Sant (1975) analysed industrial movement between British subregions from 1945 to 1971. Using cross section step wise regression analysis for four distinct time periods 1945-51, 1952-59, 1960-65 and 1966-71 and seventeen explanatory variables, he attempted to explain the pattern of the origins and destinations of movement. He found that his equations were better specified for movement from origins than movement to destinations. The origin equations showed urban employment density and the proportion of each area with urban status to have consistently significant coefficients. These indicators of congestion (typical of the periphery-centre model) tended to confirm that agglomeration diseconomies reflected in a lack of space are an important push factor in the migration process. Other factors of significance in the destination equations were labour availability, regional incentives, land availability, and the ability to satisfy the short distance move preference.

Further studies by Keeble also throw considerable light on the significance of agglomeration factors (economics and diseconomies) influencing manufacturing employment change. In a 1972 study he used gravity models to test for causes of spatial variation in the volume of movement to peripheral areas from the South East and West Midlands region, 1945 to 1965. He used labour availability as an attraction factor and distance between origin and destination as a friction factor. Labour availability was found to contribute most (86% for moves from South East, and 63% for moves from the West Midlands) to the explanation movement. The effect of distance was also significant, and was found to be greater from central conurbations than from regions as a whole. Keeble suggests that this shows that distance away from the economic centre is important for migrant firms. This distance concept could embrace a multitude of causal factors, but to some extent it is likely to be a surrogate for agglomeration advantages associated with core locations.

With Hauser (1971 and 1972) Keeble also analysed the spatial variations in manufacturing growth in Outer South East England between 1960 and 1967. The study used multiple regression analysis to study growth rates for a large number of small areas and to test a wide range of locational hypotheses, not least the effect of agglomeration economies and diseconomies. Other hypotheses under consideration were that growth was related to national demand factors, local industrial specialisation and diversification, dominance of large firms, migrant firms, market accessibility, labour availability, factory availability, proximity to communications and space perception.

Six different measures of manufacturing growth were regressed upon twenty-one explanatory variables. Population and manufacturing employment were taken as surrogates for agglomeration economies, and population density and manufacturing employment density as congestion factors in the diseconomy argument.

The results suggested that spatial variations in manufacturing change in the study region, whether measured by employment or floorspace indices, have been influenced most by variations in aggregate and specific labour availability, and in existing levels of industrial activity and specialisation.

Labour availability seems to have been important insofar as it is reflected in a population growth variable around London and (reflected in unemployment) in more peripheral locations. In addition the availability of female workers and workers with particular skills have played important roles. These factors can be seen as agglomeration advantages, although they were not the variables selected to test for agglomeration effects.

The influence of the scale of industrial activity is difficult to disentangle. However generally floorspace growth was concentrated in the larger industrial towns, while manufacturing employment growth tended to be in the smaller towns suggesting diseconomies of agglomeration for labour intensive firms. Specialisation in an area was consistently associated with decline in activity.

Looking specifically at the agglomeration variables two trends stand out for both the employment and floorspace measures of growth. Firstly industrial centres with high densities of employment were strongly associated with growth, while the larger centres tended to grow less fast than the smaller ones. Thus, overall size was more likely to be associated with diseconomies, while concentration was the important factor for agglomeration economies. This tends to suggest that improvements in communications did not increase the area over which agglomeration economies were achieved. Rather, spatial propinquity was still important in the South East in the period 1960-67. Keeble and Hauser also showed that in the New and Expanding Towns agglomeration variables had no significant influence on manufacturing growth. Perhaps this reflects the nature of moves to these towns and the maintenance of links by movers to their previous locations.

A further paper by Keeble (1979) analysed the industrial location dynamics of manufacturing employment decline in the United Kingdom from 1971-76, by subregion. He shows that many of the trends identified by Chisholm and Oeppen have been reinforced, with continuing dispersion both within and between regions. Thus, in a period of aggregate manufacturing employment decline between 1971 and 1976, it was the traditionally unindustrialised rural counties which were the only areas recording any degree of manufacturing employment growth. He attempted to explain this trend using differential shifts of manufacturing employment (1971-76) as a dependent variable in a step wise multiple regression analysis together with four independent variables. These were employment density (index for agglomeration diseconomies), investment incentives (as a proxy for government industrial location policy), residential space preference (as developed by Gould and White), and female activity rates.

The differential manufacturing shifts in employment were found to be closely related to variations in manufacturing employment density. This variable of agglomeration disadvantage accounted for 45% of the variation in rates of differential shift. This result provides support for the hypothesis that diseconomies of agglomeration in large urban centres have been a major influence on manufacturing employment decline.

Fothergill and Gudgin (1979) have also showed that the main influence upon subregional manufacturing employment change was indigenous performance and that the more rural subregions showed a marked tendency to perform better than the larger industrial conurbations through their study period of 1959 to 1975. Their analysis sought to explain regional employment trends by subregional disaggregation and the use of shift share analysis as applied to the subregional employment change. They showed that for manufacturing, service and total employment, structural influences have a far less dominant influence on employment change than the differential component - those shifts in the location of employment which cannot be attributed directly to industrial structure. In addition they found that subregion employment change had virtually no consistency within any region but rather that relative decline was taking place in London and the major conurbations, whilst the more rural subregions were experiencing relative growth in indigenous performance. In manufacturing the major processes causing growth differences between urban areas and rural areas were responsible in large part for the differences in regional growth and decline. In speculating on the causes of these urban-rural differences Fothergill and Gudgin rule out agglomeration economies quite categorically. They suggest that poor operating conditions in cities resulted in relatively poor indigenous performance and caused high closure rates and out migration. They suggest that poor premises, old capital stock, labour problems and residential preferences are all potential causes of poor performance of the cities and the conurbations. They also suggest that well established theories concerning the influence of transport costs, agglomeration economies, or centre-periphery relationships all relating to factors operating at the regional scale are not appropriate explanations of these new growth dynamics. Their analysis was all in terms of employment however, not in terms of output.

Interest in the factors affecting spatial manufacturing growth variations has not been lacking, either in the United Kingdom or the United States. Although the empirical research does not conclusively endorse the view that agglomeration economies are a major influence on growth rate variation, it leaves no doubt that agglomeration advantages and disadvantages cannot be ruled out of future causal investigations. Indeed, the overall lack of consensus on the role played by agglomeration factors in the complex dynamics of manufacturing locations should not be interpreted as a reflection of the impotence of agglomeration influence. Rather it tends to reflect the different measures used to get at the real effect of agglomeration economies and diseconomies, the different spatial units for which research has been carried out, and the changing influence of both economies of scale and external economies both over time and between industrial sectors.

3 AGGLOMERATION ECONOMIES AND INDUSTRIAL EFFICIENCY

The earlier sections of this chapter have shown that economies of agglomeration influence both industrial location decisions and regional growth, in conjunction with many other factors, but is their influence upon industrial efficiency at the heart of these processes? Among a large number of studies examining this question, Alonso (1970), Fuchs (1967) and Hoch (1972) have shown that both wages and output per worker are greater in large cities; but the cause and effect in these studies is always a little ambiguous. Are wages higher to compensate workers for the negative externalities in consumption of living in the city? Is output higher because wages are part of net output? Or is output higher because of external economies thus permitting the payment of higher wages?

Segal (1976) developed a theory of production and income to explain this variation in worker incomes and found that although returns to factors were 8% higher in the largest S.M.S.A.'s in the United States this was not due to increasing returns to scale in production, but rather was the result of economies of agglomeration which caused a shift in the aggregate production function function. (5) Sveikauskas (1975) also used United States data to show that labour productivity does vary with city size after allowing for the effect of labour quality.

In a rather dated study Brown (1972) used data from the 1948 and 1954 United Kingdom Census of Production to test whether the rate of growth of the value of net output per head was positively associated with the size of aggregation of a particular industry. He found no significant relationship. He also failed to find a significant correlation between increases in per capita output in spearate manufacturing industries and total manufacturing employment in these regions.

Brown appreciated that if there are realised productive advantages mainly external to the establishment that flow from location in a large aggregation of the relevant industry then perhaps a priori the level of output per head should be considered further. This was studied with the aid of regression analysis. Brown used an index of average output perhead for each Minimum List Heading of the Census of Production as a dependent variable with three explanatory variables: the proportion of national employment in the trade situated in the region concerned as a measure of economies external to the establishment; the average employment per establishment in the trade in the region to measure economies internal to the firm; and a series of dummy variables to test for other regional influences on productivity after allowing for scale economies.

Data was again drawn from the 1948 and 1954 Census of Production. The results for the two years were very similar and there was some evidence that external economies of scale influenced productivity. The external economy coefficient was significant and positive for clothing, leather and fur, wood and cork, and all trades together. The coefficient was positive in twelve out of sixteen equations, and near significant in a number including vehicles, metal goods, and precision instruments. The internal economy measure seemed rarely to have significant effects on productivity. The dummy variables had mixed effects with London, the West Midlands, South, East and North Midlands showing significant variation for all industries considered together.

While these results are not as conclusive as perhaps theory would suggest they should be, it should be remembered that output per head is not a perfect measure of productivity (6) and that the industrial classification is not without problems.

In a Swedish study Aberg (1973) analysed cross sectional industrial statistics for 281 regions (municipal blocks), for manufacturing industry as a whole and for selected industries. He employed regression techniques to attempt to explain empirically differences in the productivity of labour between regions and in particular the influence of agglomeration factors (using population density as a proxy), capital intensity and scale of production (using size of enterprise as a proxy). Aberg developed two different equations. The first related the productivity of labour (value added per employee) to capital intensity (capital per employee), size of enterprise, and population density. In the second, population density was replaced by a dummy variable to explain differences in productivity between groups of regions due to agglomeration effects.

Aberg found firstly that productivity did vary, region by region, and that the value added per employee was positively correlated with population density, after accounting for capital intensity and size of enterprise. It was not found however to be a strong influence. Analysis with the use of dummy variables also showed that productivity differences between regions were the result of size of plant and intensity of capital rather than external factors, but also that external factors seemed to be affecting productivity which were not explained fully by the population density proxy, or the measure of factors internal to the establishment.

These studies again tend to suggest that the influence of agglomeration economies, although only one influence among many on industrial efficiency, is nevertheless real. It is therefore of importance in understanding regional and subregional economic performance.

4 FURTHER STUDIES OF AGGLOMERATION ECONOMIES

Two further groups of studies of agglomeration economies focus on local inter-firm linkages in order to establish whether close spatial proximity of companies or plants results in important local sales and purchasing patterns and, conversely, whether strong inter-sectoral exchanges influence location patterns. These studies have had mixed success.

An obvious way to assess the importance of local inter-firm linkages, is to question industrial plants directly on the pattern of their sales and purchases. It may be of course that inertia will mean that a firm continues to have links with other local firms which do not reflect full economic efficiency; either for that firm or for a modern best practice plant. But we may expect, a priori, local linkage to be a good indicator of an agglomeration economy.

The survey results from the United Kingdom suggest that in general local linkages are not important for most industrial firms. Sales and purchases typically extend over wide geographical areas, becoming international for many larger concerns. Keeble's study (1969) of

124 firms in North West London finds this pattern; as does the survey by Economic Consultants Ltd. (1971) of 1,434 plants located in South East England. In this latter study, only 38% of all sales and 21% of all purchases were within thirty miles. Although these proportions were higher for firms located within the Greater London Council area, they were much lower in the Outer South East area, where industrial growth had been fastest; suggesting perhaps that local linkages are relatively unimportant for new and expanding firms. This result is reinforced by the study of the small East Anglian of Thetford and Haverhill by Moseley and Townroe (1973). This found that for firms newly locating in the towns local linkages were important for smaller firms in engineering and metal fabricating. This is perhaps because these firms were themselves providing something of a local service to other firms. The very detailed study of seventy-four companies in Scotland by Lever (1974) reinforces this conclusion. However the study by McDermott (1976) of the Scottish electronics industry does show the importance of purchasing linkages in Scotland (20% of purchases for Scottish controlled companies, and 11% of purchases for externally controlled companies), and of sales linkages in Scotland (40% and 19%). McDermott stresses the important subcontracting role of the indigenous firms.

Surveys in the United States, Canada and Sweden (reviewed by Pred (1976)) similarly reveal patterns of inter-firm linkage outside the local metropolitan area, with weak local linkages. However, those studies which differentiate their results by sector do reveal the importance of this type of agglomeration economy for certain categories of industry. For example, Karaska's report on the Philadelphia Regional Input Output Study (1969) shows strong local demand linkages in printing, lumber, fabricated metals, and machinery. Printing is again important in local supply linkages, together with petroleum and instruments. These results are based on input-output coefficients. These findings may be compared with the answers given in the 1966-67 London Employment Survey reported by Hoare (1975). Among the industries valuing access to suppliers as 'important and essential' were drink (58%), clothing (53%, other metals (50%), timber and furniture (47%) and leather and fur (47%). Access to markets was valued similarly by clothing (64%), timber and furniture (63%), leather and fur (62%), bricks, pottery and glass (60%), and paper, printing and publishing(59%).

These industrial breakdowns are relatively coarse, but they do point to the need for disaggregated research. There are two further general findings. Firstly, as might be expected, linkages for firms in smaller urban centres operate up the urban hierarchy. And secondly, that externalities which used to be important in the central core of larger urban areas are now available throughout those areas. Even for industries with a strong core market, such as printing and clothing, the need for a central plant location has diminished.

One problem with all survey studies of local linkage (as well as the inertia issue already touched upon) is that although only a small proportion of sales or purchases are local, that proportion may be a crucial agglomeration economy for the firm concerned. This may be especially so on the purchasing side, where there is a continual need to be in close face to face contact with a supplier. Aggregate percentages can therefore be misleading.

The second group of studies looking at local linkage has sought to infer the importance of the links by examining sectoral locational patterns, often searching for a correspondence between input-output linkages (normally obtained from a national input-output table) and the spatial correspondence of plant location patterns of two or more sectors.

Possibly the most ambitious study of spatial clustering of different industrial activities was undertaken by Bergsman, Greenston and Healy (1972) at the Urban Institute in Washington D.C.. 186 activities were clustered into forty-two mutually exclusive and collectively exhaustive groupings, using 1963 data from 203 S.M.S.A.'s in the United States as an input into three factor analyses. A subsequent paper (1975) extends the analysis to groupings of locations to allow cross classifications. All causation in the very complex sets of results is only inferred. No assessment of the importance of clustering to each sector is made. The general conclusion is important: 'The results as a whole are consistent with the idea that only a minor part of agglomeration forces act through shipment of materials or other inter-firm transactions, while rather more may depend on general characteristics of cities such as size, access to consumer markets, wages and labour force' (1975, p. 27).

Similar studies have been undertaken by Richter (1969) in the United States, by Streit (1969) in France and West Germany, and by Lever (1972) in the United Kingdom. All find distinctive spatial associations between pairs and groups of industries. However, if historical inertia is strong, mere spatial association cannot be a sure indicator of continuing inter-sectoral spatial interdependence or of the presence of currently significant agglomeration economies. These studies did not take the further step of linking the pattern of sectoral groupings to characteristics of the cities or subregions within which the groupings were located.

One possible further type of survey study which has not been attempted would be a survey of the distribution networks employed by firms in different industries, following the hypothesis that agglomeration economies are largely distribution oriented. If a group of firms uses a nationwide network of wholesalers, then there is no need for their own location to be dependent upon distribution activities. If a further group undertake distribution themselves, then they will be drawn by market factors. If a third group export most of their production, then their locations may be dominated by supply considerations such as a requirement for skilled labour.

5 CONCLUSIONS

The range of empirical work on agglomeration economies and local external economies is very wide. In many of the studies cited, assessment of the importance of external economies was not a prime focus of the work. From the variety of findings, at the risk of oversimplification, five results seem clear. First, that overall, in a highly developed and urbanised, compact economy such as the United Kingdom, local external economies are not as important as they used to be. Access per unit of expenditure stretches over greater distances than in the past. Secondly, that such economies remain important for certain sectors of industry and for certain categories of firms and plants; but that these sectors and categories remain ill-defined. Third, that urbanisation economies are more important to firms than localisation economies. Fourth, that no clear evidence has emerged of net negative local external economies to the private costs of the industrial company (although Keeble (1976, p. 74-78) argues otherwise in the case of Greater London and the West Midlands Conurbation). Fifth, that the locational impact of local external economies differs depending on whether the impact comes through from an influence on performance (efficiency and profitability), or on decisions about growth or decline, or on decisions on whether to relocate and where to locate a new investment.

In the last of the five results above, the locational impact for the simple cost minimising firm of economic theory would be the same in all three cases. But firms do not only worry about cost. Quality and reliability are as important if not more important for many firms. Others are not maximisers or minimisers at all, taking the first feasible option when choices are to be made and exhibiting inertia when it is possible without being pushed out of business. And it must not be forgotten that overshadowing all of these processes there lies the influence of public policy: the carrot and stick of regional development policy, local and national taxes and regulatory mechanisms, and the normative controls of local land use planning.

NOTES

(1) Harrison (1974) showed that the percentage of metropolitan manufacturing employment in eight large S.M.S.A.'s located in central cities fell from 81% to 61% from 1900 to 1947.

(2) Kain (1975) showed that the suburban share of manufacturing employment increased from 33% to 52% in forty S.M.S.A.'s between 1948 and 1963.

(3) A shorthand reference to a large British government survey: Department of Trade and Industry, Inquiry into Location Attitudes and Experience. Memorandum submitted to the House of Commons Expenditure Committee (1973) on Regional Development Incentives. H.C. 85-I. Session 1973-74. London H.M.S.O.

(4) Agglomeration economies as identified by Harris and Hopkins do not include economies achieved in reduced transport costs as a consequence of locating near to markets. Hence the marginal costs of transporting output are identified separately.

(5) Further analyses examining shifts in a production function come from Kawashima (1975) and Carlino (1979).

(6) Markets for labour and goods are imperfect and the value of inputs and outputs therefore vary between regions. See chapter four.

4 Measuring agglomeration economies

1 INTRODUCTION

The discussion of the previous two chapters has suggested that local external economies will influence the behaviour of an industrial company in many different ways and that these economies will arise from many different sources. Any empirical study which seeks to establish the importance of these economies for a firm or group of firms or a group of industrial establishments is therefore faced with two problems. Firstly how to measure the impact of the local external economies. Secondly how to measure the relative strength of alternative potential sources of these economies relevant to all or to a subgroup of firms or establishments in a local area, however 'local' is defined.

In this study, there was no choice of a basic impact variable. The basic direction of the study was given by the availability of figures for net output per head by industrial product group for subregions of Great Britain. This is the key impact variable and is discussed in section three of this chapter, together with two modifications which were also used. There is also a brief discussion of possible approaches to assessing the impact of agglomeration economies using production function estimation. The final part of the chapter suggests further impact variables which were not used.

Before individual variables are described however, the next section of the chapter considers the spatial base for all of the variables, the subregions of Great Britain.

2 THE SPATIAL BASE

The areas for which the data used in this study have been assembled are the sixty-one planning subregions of Great Britain as defined in 1968 (Central Statistical Office, 1969). These subregions were defined for regional planning purposes, assembled as aggregates of lower tier local authority areas (i.e. on the pre-1974 local government reform authorities: rural districts, urban districts, metropolitan boroughs and county boroughs). The definitions have changed slightly since that time (see Central Statistical Office, 1979).

The areas defined as subregions are not ideal for testing the hypotheses under consideration in this study. The subregions vary greatly in size, the largest having a population of 7,763,800 in 1968 and the smallest having a population of 84,200. More important the subregional boundaries are not functional boundaries. The central focus of the study is on agglomerations of industrial plants and on the advantages to industry of urban areas. The most appropriate spatial base would therefore be based on some concept of a set of functional urban systems, each urban area being defined on the basis of its own internal characteristics (density, commuting field etc.) and on the basis of its interrelationships with other continuous urban areas, and then linked to a hinterland. We could then compare urban area with urban area, and urban areas in a group with rural areas.

Unfortunately, urban areas in Great Britain are not spaced geographically distinct from one another. Many merge into one another when criteria such as land use or density are used, as, for example, in South East Lancashire or in the West Riding of Yorkshire. Other urban areas are essentially groups of smaller but geographically distinct towns or have a 'core' town with 'satellites'. Any classification to a statistically manageable number will produce a subgroup of towns plus hinterlands which conforms to some *a priori* notion of 'the city' relevant to the focus of this study, but the remaining areas do not conform to any built-up area stereotype. A division based on the pre-1974 local government boundaries provides both too many areas (1,732) and areas which are frequently *underbound* in both a physical and a functional sense. Attempts have been made to define a more limited number of 'city regions', for example, in the discussions leading up to the reorganisation of local government. The most appropriate of the functional definitions for this study would have been the 126 urban areas plus their commuting hinterlands, called Standard Metropolitan Labour Areas (Drewett et al., 1976). Unfortunately, the basic dependent variables are not available on this basis.

One complication with the definition of the subregions with which this study has had to work is that in a few cases Employment Exchange areas cross the subregional boundaries. It is on the basis of the Exchange areas that the Department of Employment compiles local area statistics of employment by industrial sector. However, the employment figures used in this study were taken from the work of Chisholm and Oeppen (1973). They received figures for 1959 and 1968 from the Department of Employment by subregion and by 152 minimum list headings and made adjustments in the few cases where this proved necessary.

The minimum list heading employment figures had to be collapsed into Product Groups, using the groupings listed in the appendix to this chapter. The net output per head figures from the 1968 Census of Production were supplied on a Product Group basis, Groups Four to Eighty-Six covering manufacturing industry. Where relevant, the employment data was aggregated to the Product Group level.

Many Product Groups are not represented in all subregions. In other subregions, the representation of a Product Group was so small that the Business Statistics Office could not supply the net output per head figures for fear of disclosing information relating to an individual company. Unfortunately, because the net output information was only supplied in ratio form, it was not possible with confidence to group subregions where observations had been suppressed. A cut off of a minimum of fifteen observations was used in selecting Product Groups for analysis. A total of fifty-three Product Groups was therefore considered.

3 VARIABLES REFLECTING THE IMPACT OF AGGLOMERATION ECONOMIES

(a) Net output per head

The first impact variable, a variable to reflect the relative advantages and disadvantages conferred by local external economies on a spatial grouping of industrial establishments, is the value of net output per employee by product group and subregion from the 1968 Census of Production for the United Kingdom. As indicated above, values of this variable (QQQQQQ) were provided in a set of special tabulations from the Business Statistics Office for each of the Census product groups four to eighty-six (those covering manufacturing industry). Each product group table contains values for each of sixty-one subregions within Great Britain and the eleven economic planning regions of the United Kingdom, except where an establishment of a given product group is not located in the subregion or the observation has been suppressed.

The values of net output per head have been used here as indicators of relative productivity or performance attributable to local external economies, having allowed for internal economies of scale as plant size increases. The study is therefore abstracting away from other sources of variation in net output per head. For example, within each product group there will be variations between companies and establishments in the exact nature of the products made and in the processes used. The degree of competition in the product markets might also vary, allowing higher profits to one or a subgroup of firms. For this study, these sources of variation have been assumed to be sufficiently small between subregions not to counter or mask those sources the analysis is focussing upon.

However, one potentially serious source of variation in the values of net output per head is the possibility of significant differences between subregions within a product group of the size and structure of the companies to which the establishments (on which the observations are based) belong. Larger companies will tend, other things being equal, to perform many managerial and service activities in house rather than purchasing them externally. And branch plants, compared with single plant concerns, wholly owned subsidiary companies, or corporate parent plants, will tend to receive many of these services from elsewhere in the company. (1) Unfortunately there is no data series by product group and subregion which allows these possible effects from the size and structure of companies to be included in the analysis. The work of Crum and Gudgin (1977) and others does suggest that there may be a spatial bias in these factors.

Any spatial differences in the buying in as opposed to self provision of services would matter less if the net output, as defined by the Business Statistics Office, were the same as value added, the more relevant concept for productivity measurement. Unfortunately, included in the net output figures are values for services bought in from other businesses and institutions which lie mainly outside manufacturing industry. These services are normally excluded from the concept of value added. The services include the cost of hire of plant and machinery, payments for repair and maintenance, and for advertising and selling expenses and local authority rates as well as other payments which are less closely linked to agglomeration economies (commercial insurance premiums, bank charges and licensing of motor vehicles). All of these items have to be deducted from net output to give gross value added. Gross value added is then the fund from which wages, salaries, employers' insurence and welfare contributions, taxes, interest on loans, capital expenditure (depreciation) and profits have to be met. Net output for all United Kingdom manufacturing in 1968 was 9.7% higher than the gross value added. Variations in this percentage within each product group across subregions may be quite small. Anyway, no data is available on the value of industrial services by product group and subregion in 1968 and so the net output measure used here cannot be modified.

The manner of collection of the net output figures for the 1968 industrial census is of some importance here. The Business Statistical Office accepted combined returns from multiplant firms who were unable to supply separate figures for each establishment. This had a particular effect on regional or subregional analyses because these combined returns were made irrespective of the size of the establishments or whether the establishments were located in the same region or subregion. Estimates for each area were then made for the various headings (total employment, wages and salaries, net output etc.) pro rata according to the number of operatives employed at each establishment. Further estimation had then to be made to allow for small establishments employing fewer than twenty-five persons. These establishments were not required to make detailed returns to the census. Estimations were also necessary for unsatisfactory returns. All of these estimations may clearly be a source of bias. In those subregions where there were only a few establishments employing less than twenty-five and so there was clearly no satisfactory basis for estimation, the figures were suppressed.

The industrial classification in the census is by reporting unit (normally a single establishment) on the basis of the products made in that unit. All activity in that unit is accredited to the major product group present. Industrial and subregional aggregates are therefore necessarily made up of figures for individual establishments that are somewhat dissimilar. The establishment here has been defined as the smallest unit which could provide the information normally required for an economic census. Firms were asked to exclude from their returns as far as possible particulars relating to any department not engaged in production (although head offices mainly engaged on the administration of production have been included).(2) One final point about the averaging process in compiling the data used here: it is quite likely that in many industries the variation in net output per head between establishments <u>within</u> a subregion will be greater than the variation between subregions; but there is no way of checking on this.

(b) Net output minus wages and salaries per head

Both wages rates and earnings vary across the regions and subregions of Great Britain. In 1968 the average gross weekly earnings of male manual workers were 7.9% higher in the highest paid region (South East) than in the lowest (East Anglia). The difference between the highest paid and lowest paid subregions (Merseyside and the Borders) was 37.8% for male manual workers. The differences by region are summarised in Table 4.1.

Table 4.1
Average gross weekly earnings by region in 1968

Average gross weekly earnings	Males Manual (£ per week)	Males Non manual (£ per week)	Females Manual (£ per week)	Females Non manual (£ per week)
G.B. average	23.1	31.7	11.2	15.7
Highest regional earnings	24.3 South East	34.3 South East	11.9 South East	17.0 South East
Lowest regional earnings	21.4 East Anglia	28.2 South West	10.6 East Anglia, South West, Yorks & Humberside, Wales, Scotland	14.3 North
%variation about G.B. average	+4.3 to -7.4	+8.2 to -11.0	+6.2 to -5.4	+15.9 to -8.9

Source: Department of Employment New Earnings Survey for 1968, Table 72.

Although Table 4.1 shows that inter-regional differences in earnings in 1968 were not very large, they are larger by subregion and we must suspect that they are larger still within individual product groups by subregion (although the New Earnings Survey data is not published disaggregated by area and industry simultaneously because of small sample sizes). Since payments to labour are one of the elements in value of net output of a firm or establishment, variations by area and industry in wage and salary payments will be reflected in the variation in net output per head. Within a given product group we may well consider a priori that wage payments will be higher in urban areas than rural areas, higher in large cities than small cities. These higher levels may be due to better trade union organisation in the cities, or to greater competition for labour there especially for manufacturing from the service sectors, or because urban external economies allow urban based employers in manufacturing to pay higher wages than rural based employers. Whatever the reason for this study it is clearly desirable to test an alternative dependent variable to allow for variations in wage and salary payments.

The special tabulations allow such a modification to be made. By providing a figure (by product group and subregion again) for wages and salaries as a percentage of net output, the tables allow the derivation of values of net output minus wages and salaries per employee (QQQQWS). This variable, with the caveats noted in the previous section as to the differences between net output and value added, may be taken as essentially the income to capital per employee. It is the second dependent variable.

This second variable, because of its construction, is subject to the difficulties associated with the first variable. In order of discussion these were: the unknown variation within each subregional group of establishments of this variable; possible spatial bias in the degree to which establishments in each group buy in managerial and service functions rather than purchasing from suppliers locally and nationally, accentuated by the difference between net output and value added in the U.K. Census; the problem of combined returns from multi-plant companies of the Census questionnaire, of unsatisfactory returns and of returns from small companies; and the industrial classification procedure used.

One issue which relates to both the net output per head and the net output minus wages and salaries per head variables is whether it is more appropriate to consider both numerators with the number of operatives as the denominator rather than the total number of employees. The argument for omitting the administrative, technical and clerical employees is that the spatial distribution and the wage payments of this group of employees does not follow the pattern for operatives alone and that the local external economies exert an influence primarily on the direct production operations.

This argument has not been accepted for this study. Both internal and external economies of scale arise in relation to the activities of both administrative, technical and clerical workers and operatives. External economies may particularly influence expenditures on marketing or research and development for example. And net output is the fund out of which both groups are renumerated. However in interpreting net output per head figures, it will have to be remembered that if more highly paid white collar workers in a given product group are distributed unevenly by subregion relative to operatives, then the net output per head figures will be modified. In single subregion firms this is not important for the argument about testing for the significance of local external economies; but it might weaken the tests where multi-subregional multi-plant firms are important. This will be especially true where a group of non production workers is performing services from one plant for other plants in other subregions but within the same company, such as marketing or accounting. Unfortunately no comparable data is available on this.(3) But it may be important in explaining empirical results which run against the general trend and against *a priori* exceptions as, for example, in the case of product group forty-five, Radio and Radar.

(c) The efficiency index

Values of net output per head are one measure of labour productivity. Labour productivity is often seen by economists and economic commentators as the key measure of efficiency in industrial processes. Net output per head therefore seems to be an obvious measure of efficiency, since we are interested in the extent to which agglomeration economies influence efficiency.

However care is needed when the concept of 'efficiency' is introduced. Efficiency is not the same thing as productivity. Economists are normally careful to distinguish between allocative efficiency and technical efficiency. Allocative efficiency in production focusses on the allocation of fixed values of resources between alternative processes, products and levels of output so as to maximise the value of output. Technical efficiency on the other hand relates to the way in which a firm combines inputs to achieve a given output. Economic theory normally assumes that the firm produces on a production function that yields the greatest output for a given set of inputs, where

$$Q = f(X_1, X_2 \ldots X_n) \qquad (4.1)$$

in which Q is output and $X_1 \ldots X_n$ are inputs, and f is a functional relationship relating inputs to outputs. We are interested in the impact of variation in an exogenous variable on the form and value of f.

Four problems immediately arise when we start to look for forms and values of f. There may be some inputs, X_1 which we can identify but not measure; we may be unaware of other important inputs. We cannot be sure that all firms producing a given product have equal knowledge and therefore access to the same production function. Even if equal knowledge existed, capital invested in earlier less efficient techniques has a value which only falls over time. Different vintages of capital coexist. In any empirical work there will also exist errors in measurement of both inputs and outputs, while any number of factors may cause individual firms to have short term deviations away from a long term equilibrium position.

These problems have not stopped researchers specifying alternative functional forms of production function and estimating the parameter values econometrically, at varying levels of aggregation, from the individual industrial process through the firm and the industry to the national economy. (4) An 'average' production function for a group of firms has been usual, the functional form (such as the Cobb Douglas or Constant Elasticity of Substitution models) being specified on the basis of a number of simplifying assumptions. The resulting parameter estimates reflect the technical efficiency levels of the average or representative firm (or industry or region). But micro-economic theory has normally been interested in the maximum output obtainable from given inputs at a given level of technical knowledge. This has led to the idea of 'frontier' production functions, which represent the best techniques actually in use (as opposed to the best potential techniques). The frontier function can then be used as a base against which to measure the relative efficiency of individual firms as suggested by Farrell (1957).

One recent British example of the use of a production function to examine technical efficiency across regions is the application by Dixon and Thirlwall (1975, chapter 7) of a C.E.S. function across the entire manufacturing sector in the United Kingdom. Assuming constant returns to scale, the C.E.S. production function was specified as:

$$Q = \gamma(\delta K^{-\rho} + (1-\delta) L^{-\rho})^{1/\rho} \qquad (4.2)$$

where γ is the efficiency parameter

δ is the distribution parameter

ρ is the substitution parameter

and Q, K, and L are output, capital, and labour.

Capital stock figures are not available for the United Kingdom by region and by industry. By assuming that the distribution parameter δ and the substitution parameter ρ are the same in all regions, Dixon and Thirlwall develop the relationship:

$$\log \gamma_i/\gamma_N = \frac{\Delta \log Q/L - \sigma\Delta \log (W/L)}{1 - \sigma} \qquad (4.3)$$

where $\sigma = 1/1-\rho$, the elasticity of substitution

Δ = the difference between a region and the United Kingdom

W = earnings

and σ is derived from b in the side relation

$\log Q/L = a+b \log (W/L)$

It is therefore possible to estimate values for the 'relative efficiency parameter', $\gamma i/\gamma N$ comparing each region with the United Kingdom. A development of the above relationships allows the non constant returns case to be considered. This approach does, however, require the coefficients from the side relation to be interpreted as production function parameters. This requires the normal neoclassical behavioural assumptions to be satisfied. The observations used also need to reflect a production surface; and it may well be that observations within each industry do not come from the same production surface. Further, firms may not be using an optimal process at ruling input combinations; and the wage rate may not be exogenous. There may therefore be specification error in the equations used. (Dixon and Thirlwall, 1975, App. 1).

Problems of specification and identification occur in all empirical studies using production functions as a method of measuring relative efficiencies. Aggregation is also a prime conceptual difficulty. Indeed Fisher (1969) suggested that where aggregate output and labour variables were formed as arithmetic sums (assuming them to both be homogeneous), an aggregate capital variable would exist only if the underlying production function exhibited constant returns to scale, and capital vintages differed only through the impact of disembodied capital augmenting technical progress, such that different capital goods in different firms could be represented as more or less the same thing.

These various difficulties, both conceptual and empirical, with the estimation of production functions as a route to the consideration of the relative efficiency of subgroups of firms, and the limitations of net output per head as a measure of labour productivity alone, suggest the need to search for an alternative method of measuring relative efficiency differentials. The alternative method used in this study has been a modification of a generalised productivity index, taken from Kendrick (1961).

In simplified notation the index for a given industry in one subregion is:

$$\pi_i = \frac{Qi}{Q} / \left(\alpha \frac{Li}{L} + \beta \frac{Ki}{K}\right) \qquad (4.5)$$

where Qi, Li and Ki are the values of net output and the labour and capital inputs of the industry in subregion i, and Q, L and K are the values for the industry nationally, while α and β are the national shares of labour and capital in income. The index therefore relates the net output in a subregion as a proportion of the national net output of the industry in relation to the share of that subregion in the utilisation of primary inputs in relation to the inputs used by the industry nationally. The average level of efficiency of each industry at the national level is obviously unity. A region or subregion has a higher than average (national) level of efficiency if $\pi i > 1$ and vice versa if $\pi i < 1$.

This index is fully developed by Laos (1977, ch. 4). He refers to a number of assumptions which lie behind its construction:

(i) that outputs and inputs can be measured in a meaningful way.

(ii) that the fixed input output coefficients of production may vary from region to region both within the same process and for several processes used in manufacturing a given product.

(iii) that the unitary price of net output, the depreciation rate, the wage rate and the net profit rate paid by a given process are identical for all firms utilising such a process if the firms are located within the same region.

(iv) that an overall index of relative efficiency of each process in each region can be viewed as a weighted average of the partial efficiency measures of the requirement of each input per unit of output.

(v) that the overall level of efficiency of an industry producing several products in a given region can be measured as a weighted average of the efficiency achieved in the production of each product, the weights being the relative importance of combined inputs utilised in the production of each product in relation to the total amount of inputs into the industry in the region.

These assumptions and the derivation by Laos provide a different route to the same end than the development by Kendrick (1961) (and, later, Denison (1967)). The earlier models require smooth substitutability between labour and capital and the equalisation of the marginal products of each factor, and so the assumption of perfect competition in both product and factor markets becomes crucial. They also require constant returns to scale and productivity or efficiency change that is technically neutral, i.e. not affecting the marginal products of the factors. These assumptions are not required here.

However, the index is limited in its construction by an underlying assumption that average (national) product and factor prices are used in the measurement. The relative efficiencies of an industrial sector in different regions might change in their rankings if changes in relative factor and product prices were introduced. From the discussion earlier in this chapter, this is probably a strong assumption only in respect of the labour factor. Even there Brown (1972) has shown that inter-industry variance in earnings in 1961 was nearly three times as great as inter-regional variance. The index is also limited by only considering the labour and capital inputs. The fact that other variables may also influence differences in regional levels of efficiency is the key to the use of the index as a third dependent variable in the regression tests reported on in chapter eight.

In order to be able to derive values of the index of efficiency from the data available, one further assumption has to be added and the form of the index modified. If we divide the right hand side of equation 4.5 top and bottom by Li/L we obtain

$$\pi_i = \frac{qi}{q}/(\alpha + \beta\frac{ki}{k}) \qquad (4.6)$$

where $qi = \frac{Qi}{Li}$, $q = Q/L$, $ki = \frac{Ki}{Li}$ and $k = K/L$

Information is available on qi, q, αi and α from the special tabulations of the Business Statistics Office.

If Wi is the wage and salary bill for the industry in subregion i and ri is the cost of capital, then the share of labour in net output in the subregion:

$$\alpha i = \frac{Wi}{Qi} = 1\text{-}r\,\frac{Ki}{Qi} = 1 - \frac{riKi}{qiLi}$$

now $ki = \frac{Ki}{Li} = (1\text{-}\alpha i)\frac{qi}{ri}$

and $k = \frac{K}{L} = (1\text{-}\alpha)\frac{q}{r}$

so $\frac{ki}{k} = \frac{(1\text{-}\alpha i)}{(1\text{-}\alpha)}\,\frac{qi}{q}$ if we assume ri = rj = r

now substituting into equation 4.6 with $\beta = 1\text{-}\alpha$,

$$\pi i = \frac{qi}{q}/(\alpha + (1\text{-}\alpha i)\frac{qi}{q}) = 1/(\alpha\frac{q}{qi} + 1 - \alpha i) \qquad (4.7)$$

This form of the index of efficiency, 4.7, has been used as the third impact variable (EFFINN). It makes the assumption that the cost of capital is uniform across regions within each industry, and it ignores quality differences in the factor inputs, referring only to the use made of those inputs.

4 FURTHER POSSIBLE IMPACT VARIABLES

The performance of individual companies has eventually to be assessed on the bottom line of the profit and loss account: the post tax profit available for distribution to shareholders or for retention in the business for net investment. In the medium and long term, the behavioural impact of any source of spatial advantage accruing to a company vis-a-vis its competitors has to work through this net profit figure. Why not use this figure to compare the impact of agglomeration economies on firms or groups of firms?

There are three reasons why net or residual profit figures are unsuitable for this type of study. Firstly, differing accounting conventions, especially in respect of stock valuation and the depreciation of fixed capital, may mean that like is not being compared with like, firm to firm. The tax liabilities in a given accounting year may also not reflect the trading experience of the relevant tax year (usually a year earlier). Capital gains and losses, and the associated tax liabilities, also do not reflect efficiency in manufacture and trading. Secondly, reported profits relate to the company rather than the establishment. Many companies are multiplant, multisubregional concerns. And the third but related reason is that the Census of Production does not collect the relevant balance sheet details. Its focus is very much on the pattern of inputs and outputs associated with production at the establishment level. Sources and uses of funds in companies are surveyed in a separate exercise by the Business Statistics Office. There is no available breakdown by subregion and industrial sector.

The Census of Production does collect information on capital expenditure. This might form a suitable impact variable, the argument being that agglomeration economies result in some locations being more attractive for new investment than others. One difficulty here is the high degree of locational inertia of established industrial plants; and the greater proportion of investment which is undertaken within existing plants rather than in new plants. Therefore the analyst would not know whether a relatively high rate of investment in a given industry in a given subregion was due to the attractions provided by local external economies or whether it was due to the relative concentration of existing plants in the industry in the subregion in which investment was taking place incrementally, the relative concentration of plants being due to locational factors which may or may not still be operating.

Furthermore, industrial investment in the United Kingdom has been subject to two forms of locational control and to locational subsidies. In 1968 any industrial investment in buildings of over 5,000 square feet required an industrial development certificate from the Board of Trade (now the Department of Industry) before the company could then apply for land use planning permission from the relevant local government authority. These two controls has three major effects at that time. (5) The i.d.c. control was in part designed to encourage new plants to locate in the Assisted Areas. A further encouragement in the form of grants and investment depreciation allowances was (and is) also available in those Areas, together with advance factory buildings and serviced industrial sites provided by the central government. The second effect was to restrain industrial development in rural areas, particularly in the rural hinterlands of towns and conurbations. The third was to slow changes in land use within towns and cities. Each of these policy induced effects would have the effect of masking or distorting the unrestrained impact of agglomeration economies on the locational pattern of investment.

The three policy influences on investment patterns have also strongly influenced a further possible contender as an impact variable for this study: variation in the growth of employment by industrial sector and by subregion. Although the i.d.c. policy was, and is, focussed on industrial floorspace, the essential rationale of the policy lies in influencing the locational pattern of new job creation in manufacturing. Similarly, the Assisted Area subsidies. And land use planning policies, while concerned with amenity and environmental impace, are also very much focussed on the spatial distribution of jobs. A major physical planning impact at the subregional scale on the distribution of jobs in the 1960's in Great Britain resulted from the growth of the New Town and Expanding Town schemes. For example, between 1959 and 1966, the eight New Towns and two Expanded Town schemes in the Outer Metropolitan subregion of South East England received a net increase of 51,000 jobs in manufacturing, or 27% of the total net manufacturing growth in the Outer Metropolitan Area (Keeble, 1976, p. 85).

Variations in the growth of net output by industrial sector and by subregion would form a more appropriate variable than one based on the growth in employment, but that also would suffer from the various policy influences. Figures are not available for either the growth of output or investment on the relevant spatial basis.

5 CONCLUSION

This chapter has discussed the areas on which the statistical analysis of the later chapters is based. It has also introduced the three variables chosen to reflect inter-area differences in the impact of local external economies on the industrial sectors considered: net output per head, net output minus wages and salaries per head, and the index of efficiency. The next chapter introduces the variables which were considered as possibly reflecting the various sources and intensities of the main categories of local external economy.

NOTES

(1) Crum and Gudgin (1977), in their extensive study of non production workers in United Kingdom manufacturing industry, found that (p. 30) not only does the proportion of non production workers fall significantly, having standardised for industrial structure, in the Development Area regions, particularly in those parts of those regions outside the conurbations; but also that (p. 93) branch plants had lower average proportion of non production workers than production sites which included head offices. The distribution of head offices is biased towards larger cities and to the South East of the United Kingdom. Branch plants import services to a much greater extent than they export them; and the extent of their import increases with the distance of the

branch from London, whereas the quantity of services exported decreases. The degree of centralisation of services depends upon the corporate structure of the company: subsidiary type or branch type (p. 95). The number of specialised non production activities increases with corporate size, but the proportion of non production workers on average declines with size with economies of scale in administration (pp. 87-91).

(2) Changing definitions, usages and concepts in measuring net output and value added in the United Kingdom Census of Production have recently been explained by the Chief Statistician (Mitchell, 1978).

(3) Only the survey data from Crum and Gudgin (1977, ch. 7).

(4) The most important review of this work is by Walters (1963). More recent reviews are by Heathfield (1971) and Bosworth (1977).

(5) These policies are discussed at length in Keeble (1976), especially chapter eight.

APPENDIX

Product groups defined by 1968 standard industrial classification

Product groups used in the study

Product Group Number	Description	S.I.C. Minimum List Heading	1968 Input-Output Industry Group
	FOOD		
4	Grain milling products and animal and poultry foods and feeding stuffs	211,219	6 + 7 (part)
5	Bread, flour confectionery and biscuits	212,213	7 (part)
6	Bacon, meat and fish products	214	11 (part)
8	Cocoa, chocolate and sugar confectionery	217	9
9	Fruit and vegetable products	218	11 (part)
11	All other food products	215,229	11 (part)
	DRINK		
12	Beer and malt	231	13 (part)
14	Soft drinks, British wines, cider and perry	232,239	12 + 13 (part)
	CHEMICALS AND ALLIED PRODUCTS		
23	Synthetic resins, rubber and plastics	276	22
25	Other chemicals	271, 277, 278, 279, (part)	17 + 23 + 24 + 25 (part)
	METAL MANUFACTURE		
26	Iron and steel	311, 312, 313	26 + 27
27	Aluminium	321	28
28	Copper, brass and other base metals	322, 323	29

Product Group Number	Description	S.I.C. Minimum List Heading	1968 Input-Output Industry Group
	MECHANICAL ENGINEERING GOODS		
29	Agricultural machinery (except tractors)	331	30
30	Metal working machine tools	332	31
31	Pumps, valves, compressors and fluid power equipment	333	32
34	Construction and earthmoving equipment	336	35 (part)
35	Mechanical handling equipment including powered industrial trucks and tractors	337	35 (part)
37	Industrial plant and constructional steelwork	341	38
38	Other non-electrical machinery	339	37
39	Other mechanical engineering	342, 349	39
	INSTRUMENT ENGINEERING GOODS		
40	Photographic and document copying equipment, surgical instruments and appliances, watches and clocks	351, 352, 353	40 (part)
41	Scientific and industrial instruments, and systems including computers and peripheral equipment not separable from industrial control systems	354	40 (part)
	ELECTRICAL ENGINEERING GOODS		
42	Electrical machinery	361	41
45	Radio, radar and electronic capital goods, broadcast receiving and sound reproducing equipment, radio and electronic components, telegraph and telephone apparatus	363, 364 365, 367	43 (part)

Product Group Number	Description	S.I.C. Minimum List Heading	1968 Input-Output Industry Group
	ELECTRICAL ENGINEERING GOODS		
46	Domestic electrical appliances	368	44
47	Miscellaneous electrical goods	369	45
	SHIPBUILDING AND MARINE ENGINEERING		
48+	Shipbuilding and ship repairing	370	46
49	Marine engineering		
	VEHICLES		
50	Motor vehicles	380, 381	47 + 48
52 to 55	Aero engines, air fumes, air cushion vehicles, aerospace equipment	383	49
	METAL GOODS NOT ELSEWHERE SPECIFIED		
57	Engineers' small tools and gauges	390	51
59	Hand tools and implements, cutlery and plated table-ware, bolts, nuts, screws, rivets, etc., wire manufacture, jewellery and other metal products	391, 392 393, 394 396, 399	52 + 53 +54 + 56
	TEXTILES		
61	Yarn and thread of cotton, flax and manmade fibres	412	58 (part)
63	Woollen and worsted products	414	59
64	Hosiery and other knitted goods	417	60
67	Other textile manufactures including asbestos products	415, 416, 418, 421, 422, 429	62 + 64

Product Group Number	Description	S.I.C. Minimum List Heading	1968 Input-Output Industry Group
	CLOTHING AND FOOTWEAR		
68	Leather, leather goods and fur	431, 432 433	65
69	Men's and boy's tailored outerwear	442	66 (part)
70	Women's and girl's tailored outerwear	443	66 (part)
71	Dresses, lingerie, infants' wear	445	66 (part)
72	Other clothing, including waterproof outerwear, overalls, men's outerwear, corsetry, gloves, hats, etc.	441, 444 446, 449	66 (part)
73	Footwear	450	67
	BRICKS, POTTERY, GLASS, CEMENT, ETC.		
74	Bricks, foreclay and refactory goods	461	68
76	Glass and glass fibre	463	69 (part)
78	Other building materials and abrasives	469	71
	TIMBER, FURNITURE, ETC.		
79	Furniture, upholstery, bedding and soft furnishings	472, 473	72
80	Timber and miscellaneous wood manufactures	471, 474 475, 479	73
	PAPER, PRINTING AND PUBLISHING		
81	Paper and board	481	74
82	Products of paper and board	482, 483 484	75 + 76
83	Newspapers, periodicals and other printed and published matter	485, 486 489	77

Product Group Number	Description	S.I.C. Minimum List Heading	1968 Input-Output Industry Group
	OTHER MANUFACTURES		
84	Rubber manufactures	491	78
85	Linoleum, plastics floor covering, leather cloth etc., plastic moulding and fabricating	492, 496	79 + 80 (part)
86	Other manufactures including brushes and brooms, toys, games, children's carriages, sports equipment and stationers' goods	493, 494 495, 499	80 (part)

B Product groups not used in the study

Product Group Number	Description	S.I.C. Minimum List Heading	1968 Input-Output Industry Group
7	Sugar	216	8
10	Vegetable and animal oils and fats	221	10
13	Spirits	239 (part)	13 (part)
15	Cigarettes, cigars and tobacco etc.	240	14
16	Hard coke and manufactured fuel etc.	261	15
17	Petroleum products	262	16 (part)
18	Lubricating oils and greases	263	16 (part)
19	Pharmaceutical chemicals and preparations	272	18
20	Toilet preparations and perfumery	273	19
21	Paint	274	20
22	Soap and detergent	275	21
24	Polishes, adhesives, gelatine, etc.	279 (part)	25 (part)
32	Industrial and marine engines	334	33
33	Textile machinery and accessories	335	34
36	Office machinery	338	36
43	Insulated wires and cables	362	42
44	Electronic computers	366	43 (part)
51	Motor cycles, tricycles and pedal cycles	382	50 (part)
56	Locomotives, railway wagons etc.	384, 385	50 (part)
58	Cans and metal boxes	395	55

Product Group Number	Definition	S.I.C. Minimum List Heading	1968 Input-Output Industry Group
60	Manmade fibres	411	57
62	Cloth and piece goods of cotton, linen, silk and non made fibre	413	58 (part)
65	Carpets	419	61
66	Textile finishing	423	63
75	Pottery and china	462	69 (part)
77	Cement	464	70

Sources: Business Statistics Office, Report on the Census of Production 1968: Summary Tables, H.M.S.O., 1974, Appendix.

Central Statistical Office, Input-Output Tables for the United Kingdom 1968, H.M.S.O., 1973, Appendix D.

5 Measuring the sources of agglomeration economies

1 INTRODUCTION

In chapter four we saw that agglomeration economies will change the cost and/or the profit schedules of firms differentially over space, the change being reflected in the productivity of factors or in some index of overall efficiency. In chapter two it was suggested that these economies will originate in a number of different attributes of the firm and the local environment within which the production process takes place. Any empirical study which seeks to link or associate variations in those attributes with variations in the productivity or efficiency of subgroups of firms or industrial plants faces two problems. The first is theoretical and classificatory: to catch on an a priori basis the full range of attributes or sources of agglomeration economy. This problem was addressed in chapter two and in the review of past studies in chapter three. The second problem is how to measure the attributes.

This chapter follows the classification scheme of chapter two, distinguishing internal economies of scale from the two categories of external economies of scale: economies of localisation and urbanisation economies. Internal economies of scale relate to the size of the industrial establishment, economies of localisation are specific to a given industrial sector but not to other sectors, while urbanisation economies are local external economies benefitting all sectors of industry (here manufacturing only). The various variables considered and tested in each of these three categories are discussed in each of the next three sections of the chapter.

For each of the three categories of agglomeration economy a number of alternative variables were considered. This was partly in response to the past theoretical and empirical literature on agglomeration economies. But it was more in response to the knowledge that most of the variables considered are proxies for underlying unobservable variables. As proxies, the variables only approximately reflect the true variation in the sources of cost reduction or profit increase in each category. There may well be therefore a choice of proxies available, depending upon the data sources, with a good a priori case for each one. Or alternatively, a case for using more than one together, if it is considered that each proxy reflects a different aspect of the particular source of economy under consideration.

The degree of conceptual overlap of alternative measures of each source of economy will vary considerably and may be freely argued over. For testing hypotheses as to the significance of the import of those alternatives using multiple regression analysis, however, there is a further problem: a statistical problem. Many of the alternative variables considered will change in value in step with one another across the local areas, the subregions, considered. They will be highly intercorrelated and so give rise to the problem of collinearity if used together in a regression equation. Indeed, collinearity will be a problem not only for alternative variables introduced to reflect a single source of agglomeration economy (e.g. the labour pool), but it will also be a problem between variables reflecting different sources of agglomeration economy (e.g. labour pool versus local services). The variables chosen for the regression analysis are therefore selected in part to minimise collinearity but at the same time to maintain a consistency with the hypotheses being tested as to the different sources of economy. An inevitable compromise has to be introduced. This will influence the interpretation of the results of chapter eight.

The statistical importance of the compromise will vary, product group to product group. The variables which are specific to a given product group reflecting internal economies of scale and economies of localisation will vary in their degree of correlation with the urbanisation economy variables. Rather than modify the variables selected for regression analysis in each product group to take account of this collinearity, the selection has been kept constant across all product groups for consistency. Possible bias in the significance tests will be noted as the results for each product group are interpreted.

In the last chapter the problem of aggregation was touched upon. Each observation of the dependent or impact variables is generated by a group of unspecified size of industrial establishments in each product group and each subregion. The observation is an average for the group. There is no way of telling whether the in-group variation is greater than the variation between groups in different subregions. A similar problem arises with the source variables. The internal economy of scale variables are subregional group averages. The external economy of scale variables relate to each subregion as a whole, as a subregional attribute. The aggregation problem here is that the variables considered (except for a variable reflecting the proportion of each subregion that may be classified as urban) all treat each subregion as homogenous spatially. This can be interpreted as meaning that there is an underlying assumption in all the analysis that each establishment in a product group in a subregion has equal access to, or ability to be influenced by, a given subregional attribute. For example, each establishment in product group sixty-three, Woollen and Worsted Products, has an equal access to the labour pool in the subregion. Clearly, the degree to which the spatial distribution of the establishments involved (which is unknown) coincides with the spatial distribution of the attributes (which could only be known, if at all, with a lot of extra research time) of the subregion will vary with both the product group and the subregion. For large spatially heterogeneous subregions this lack of spatial correspondence may be large enough to influence the significance which can be attached to the results of the hypothesis testing. This analysis assumes not; remembering in the interpretation of the results that the considerations of 'on average' and of probability lie behind the statistical associations discovered.

2 INTERNAL ECONOMIES OF SCALE

The unit costs of many production processes fall with increasing levels of output. With a given investment in plant and equipment, the costs will fall as more of the potential output of the investment is realised, as capacity utilisation increases. Unit costs may also fall as the work force learns to use the equipment more efficiently. Neither of these effects can be captured in the empirical measures used in this study. But unit costs may also fall, and net output per worker increase, as the scale of the investment in a given plant or process increases. Without increasing the intensity of capital per unit of output, a given technology may allow increases in output per unit of input as output rises. Changes in technology normally reinforce this effect. We can measure differences in the average size of plant or establishment by product group in each subregion to reflect these internal scale economies.

Unfortunately the data available do not allow a distinction to be made between those internal economies of scale which originate in the plant or process and those which occur at the scale of the firm or enterprise. A large company has a number of advantages over a small company which result directly from its size. It may be able to borrow money more cheaply; to fully employ specialist equipment and personnel who would be underemployed in a small firm; to purchase supplies in bulk at a discount; to provide specialist training for its workforce; or to restrict credit to suppliers while limiting credit to customers. In the longer term, the larger firm may have technological advantages. It is not possible to diagnose the extent to which these scale economies are realised separately or collectively subregion by subregion. Many companies anyway have plants in more than one subregion.

Two measures of average plant size are available: net output per establishment and the average number employed per establishment. Both measures are simple averages; nothing is known of the shape of the distributions. But both may be regarded as measures of the scope for internal economies of scale. The net output measure of plant size will of course, be influenced by relative prices. It is not a physical measure. This would lead some to a preference for the employment measure. But scale economies are frequently reflected in a more efficient use of the labour input per unit of output. After experimentation on the assumption (e.g. from the work of Pratten, 1971) that internal economies of scale are rarely linear, the log of net output per establishment was adopted as the first independent variable (LNNNQQ).

3 LOCALISATION ECONOMIES

It is difficult to identify unambiguously the source of those agglomeration economies which are specific to a particular industry. A given pool of labour with a particular mix of occupational skills may serve as a local externality for more sectors than the one which primarily uses those skills. A specialist service, although initially tailored for one industry, may in fact supply several. The distinction between economies of localisation and urbanisation is not watertight. Nor is the distinction with internal economies of scale. Large firms may be able to provide specialist services etc. for themselves, thus 'internalising' what is otherwise an external economy for small firms.

Variables measuring economies of localisation may be split into two groups: those which serve as proxies for the suspected existence of sources of economies of localisation and those which measure directly or indirectly the link between a given sector and the source of the economy. In the first group we might include a measure of the scale of the sector in a given subregion e.g.

(i) Labour employed in the product group

(ii) Number of establishments in the product group

(iii) Gross or net output in the product group

Shefer (1973), for example, uses a scale parameter in a production function approach, suggesting that (p. 57) 'Localisation economies ... are the efficiency in production attributed to the size of the industry (all firms) in a S.M.S.A.'. In the present study the number employed in the product group was tested as a variable in a subgroup of product groups. (1) Correlations with the dependent variables were surprisingly low, and the coefficients in the regression models tested were not significant. This test is described in chapter seven. The variable was therefore dropped from the analysis.

A further variable which has been suggested as a proxy for economies of localisation (or in aggregate for urbanisation economies) is land rents. Edel (1972), for example, in arguing that the benefits of agglomeration tend to accrue to the land owner, the entrepreneur and the upper income household while the poor bear the brunt of the costs, suggests that net local external economies of scale are capitalised in land values. The argument really only holds up however, if purchasers or renters of land can fully evaluate both the external economies and diseconomies associated with a given site. Barr (1972) extends the argument to the general proposition of economies of scale in cities. The labour demand of each individual firm is so small that changing its own employment does not yield an internal scale effect. But if all firms increase output and employment, then externalities are enhanced and further activity is stimulated. So there may be increasing returns to scale in an industry (or all industries in aggregate) even when there are constant returns to the individual firm. No information on land rents and capital values is available by sector and by city.

The second group of variables reflecting economies of localisation are direct and indirect measures rather than proxies. An input-output table allows us to see the pattern of input and output linkages of each product group with all other product groups. Ideally for the analysis undertaken here, we would require an input-output table for each subregion. We could then follow the analysis (described in chapter three) of Richter (1969) and Streit (1969). High levels of linkage with other industries within the same subregion would reflect economies of localisation for a given product group within one subregion rather than another. A refinement of this would be a form of gravity model to account for distances between the plants of the industries concerned. On the output side, for example, this could be a variation of the income potential model:

$$V_i^h = K \sum_{j=1}^{J} \frac{C_{ij}^h \, M_j^h}{(d_{ij})^{\beta}}$$

where

V_i^h is an index of local market potential for industry i in subregion h

C_{ij}^h is the input-output coefficient of sales from industry i to industry j in subregion h

M_j^h is some measure of the purchasing power or size of industry j in subregion h

d_{ij} is the average distance between establishments in industry i and industry j in subregion h

K, β are constants

Unfortunately, not only are measures of distances between industrial establishments not available: nor are subregional input-output tables. However, input-output coefficients are available at a national level for 1968 in the United Kingdom to show the pattern of purchases by each industrial sector from each other industrial sector. It was therefore possible to construct an index of potential local industrial input linkages for each industry in each subregion weighting the proportion of the purchasers of industry j from industry i nationally by the size (number employed) of industry i in the subregion:

$$A_j^h = \sum_{i=1}^{N} \frac{X_i^h}{\sum_{h=1}^{T} X_i^h} a_{ij}$$

where

A_j^h is the index of potential local inter industrial input linkages for industry j in subregion h.

a_{ij} is the national input-output coefficient of industry i in relation to industry j.

X_i^h is employment in industry i in subregion h (i = 1 ..... N)

$\sum_{h=1}^{T} X_i^h$ is employment in industry i across all subregions (h = 1 ..... T).

The variable A_i^h could not be calculated for all of the fifty-three product groups used in the analysis because of incompatible industrial classifications in the data sources. (2) The variable was constructed for an initial ten product groups, all chosen in the expectation of finding important local linkages. (3) However in all ten groups the correlations with the three dependent variables were so low that the variable was subsequently dropped from the analysis.

Two further possible measures of economies of localisation were referred to at the beginning of this section. One was the size of the pool of labour skills specific to a product group in a given subregion. A weighted index could be prepared reflecting the skill mix used in the industry locally or on average nationally. Such an index would fail to reflect however the ease with which employees in certain occupation groups can transfer to other occupations. The second measure was some form of index of non industrial services specific to a product group in a subregion. Unfortunately for both of these measures the relevant information is not available by product group at the subregional level.

4 URBANISATION ECONOMIES

One approach to measuring the importance of all forms of agglomeration economy on a given point in space has been suggested by Richardson (1973) in his index of agglomeration potential. Agglomeration economies and diseconomies are not only multidimensional but have differential patterns of distance decay. The agglomeration potential of centre j on location i, ${}^{i}Z^{j}$ may therefore be represented by:

$$ {}^{i}Z^{j} = G_1 \, A_{j_1}^{\alpha 1} \; A_{j_2}^{\alpha 2} \; ..... \; A_{j_n}^{\alpha n}, \; d_{ij_1}^{-\beta 1} \; d_{ij_2}^{-\beta 2} \; ..... \; d_{ij_x}^{-\beta x} $$

where

G is a constant

A_{jn} is a source of agglomeration economy n in centre j

d_{ij_x} is some measure of distance between i and j

α, β are weights.

Richardson does not however provide guidance as to how the A's shall be measured, and the detailed distance information for d_{ij} is not normally available. Urbanisation economies, which are sources of increased economic efficiency for all sectors of industry, have therefore to be measured by variables acting as proxies for each source of economy. The variables reflect an attribute or characteristic not of a point in space but of an urban area; or in the case of this analysis, a subregion. Each variable discussed in this section is not specific to a product group but is general to a subregion and so may be seen as reflecting variations in a specified characteristic of the sixty-one subregions.

(a) Labour force variables

The first group of variables tested are based on the proposition that the local pool of labour is an important agglomeration economy for manufacturing companies:

(i) The number of employees in manufacturing industry in the subregion (XXXXXI). This general variable gives a non specific indicator of the relative number of employees in the subregion. There will, of course, be some transferability within and between occupations from the non manufacturing sectors: agriculture and mining, construction, the utilities and the service industries. (4) This variable was also used in a non linear logarithmic form.

(ii) The total monthly unemployed 1966-70, average of June and December (XXXXXX8). A more direct measure of the pool of available labour.

(iii) The number of skilled manual workers, 1966 (SKILMN) and the number of semi skilled manual workers, 1966 (SEMSKL). Many location surveys have suggested that the search for skilled labour is a key element in the choice of a new site. Any restraint on the supply of skilled labour may place a production plant at a disadvantage with its competitors. This source of urbanisation economy may be particularly important for smaller companies.

(iv) Economically active males, 1966 (ECACTM) and Economically active females, 1966 (ECACTF). The proportion of male and female employees varies considerably between product groups. These two variables are extensions of the first variable of this group and were included to test for the relative importance of the sex of the labour pool.

(v) Female activity rate, 1966 (XXXXX5). Reserves of female labour are not often registered as unemployed but may nevertheless be important to particular product groups.

(vi) Male and female earnings, 1968 (XXXXX6, XXXXX7). A further attribute of local labour pools, although these variables have to be used with care given the nature of the dependent variables.

(vii) The percentage unemployment rate, 1966-70, average of June and December (XXXXX9). This could be seen either as a measure of labour availability; or as a measure of the degree to which a subregion was a problem area, reflecting an older capital stock and a lower quality of public infrastructure capital.

(viii) The percentage of employment in that part of the subregion classified as Assisted Area in 1966 (XXXX10). A variable reflecting the disadvantages associated with industrial structural decline, low levels of past investment and/or locational disadvantage.

(b) Access to services

Industrial companies purchase an extremely wide variety of services of all sorts: legal, financial, technical, research, marketing, etc. It is difficult to reflect either the pattern of services actually purchased, or those services available in a local area for purchase if required, in a single variable. However, figures of employment in each subregion in a number of service trades in 1968 are available. These were used both individually and also collectively in a principal component to reflect a third group of urbanisation economies.

(i) Employment in m.l.h. 703 Road Haulage Contracting (5) (RDHAUL).

(ii) Employment in m.l.h. 709 Miscellaneous Transport Services and Storage (MSTRAN).

(iii) Employment in m.l.h. 810 Wholesale Distribution (WHOLES).

(iv) Employment in m.l.h. 832 Dealing in other Industrial Materials and Machinery (DEALMT).

(v) Employment in m.l.h. 860 Insurance, Banking and Finance (INSURN).

(vi) Employment in m.l.h. 871 Accounting Services (ACCOUN).

(vii) Employment in m.l.h. 873 Legal Services (LEGAL).

(viii) Employment in m.l.h. 879 Other Professional and Scientific Services (PROFES).

Richardson (1973) has suggested that the growth in services might be used as a proxy measure of agglomeration economics. Measures of the growth of all of the above 1959-68 are available and were used as a third group of variables. However, the direction of causation is not clear. Agglomeration economies may be more favourable in a given subregion because of recent strong growth in these services. Alternatively the growth in services may have been in response to economies of agglomeration specific to the services.

(c) Size of agglomerations

The subregions used in this study vary greatly not only in size but also in their urban structure. Insofar as size and structure influence the availability of local external economies to an industrial establishment, then it is important to include appropriate variables. It is, however, difficult to prejudge just which variables are appropriate.

(i) Population, 1966 (POPULN). A population variable may be interpreted in a number of different ways. It is one measure of the extent of the local market. It is also a catch all size variable insofar as sources of agglomeration economy increase with size. It is a fairly direct reflection of those indirect agglomeration economies which might be associated with good cultural and recreational facilities (although this interpretation can be discounted here given the other variables to be tested). Finally, population size has been suggested as a possible measure of agglomeration diseconomies (by Baumol, 1967) when used in an urban rather than a regional context. The variable was used in both linear and logarithmic forms.

(ii) Urban population density, 1966 (XXXXX2). Average density is one measure of the urban hierarchy of a subregion. Again a log transform was used. It was tried by Carlino (1978) but dropped in favour of population scale.

(iii) Size of subregion (XXXXX4). This variable, measured as an average radius in miles, reflects the broad spatial configuration of the subregion.

(d) Other characteristics of the subregions

(i) The percentage of the region classified as urban, 1966 (XXXXX3). This is an imperfect variable based on the administrative division between rural district councils and urban district and borough councils.

(ii) A rural-urban dummy variable (URBRUR). A subset of subregions was defined as rural using the 'semi rural' and 'rural' divisions adopted in the classification of subregions by Fothergill and Gudgin (1979, p. 182).

(iii) Net migration flow, 1966 (MIGRAT). Areas of industrial decline and of poor competitive structure are frequently characterised by out migration. This migration is typically selective, the young, the educated and the enterprising moving out. Out migration becomes thus a source of urban diseconomy. The converse is true of in migration, except where the flow is so great as to lead to congestion. This form of congestion will have a greater impact on households than on companies.

The variables in these four groups reflecting sources of urbanisation economies do not, of course, constitute an exhaustive list. There is no variable which directly reflects the efficiency of local public services. There is no variable, other than the population and unemployment variables, which directly reflects urban diseconomies. In the final group there is no variable which reflects the spatial distribution of each urban centre within the subregion or the size hierarchy of the centres. And behind all of the subregional characteristics, there is no reflection in the measurements of the fact that each subregion borders other subregions. Commuting flows and patterns of access to services run across subregional boundaries. A glance at the map of the subregions shows how this might be important, for example, in North West England. All of those additional considerations could be built into new variables with enough data and enough research time.

5 CONCLUSION

This chapter has introduced the variables used in this study to measure three aspects of agglomeration economies: internal economies of scale, economies of localisation and urbanisation economies. The list of variables is long. Many variables will be dropped from the analysis after an initial examination of the correlations with the dependent variables except where there is a strong a priori reason for its retention in one of the eventual regression models tested. The correlations are examined in chapter seven. But firstly in the next chapter the spatial distribution of both the dependent and independent variables is considered.

NOTES

(1) The data on employment by industry by subregion were kindly provided by Professor Michael Chisholm of the University of Cambridge. These are classified by the 1958 Standard Industrial Classification (see Chisholm and Oeppen, 1973) and so have to be transformed where possible to the 1968 groupings.

(2) The 1968 Census of Production Product Groups bring together the minimum list headings of the 1968 Standard Industrial Classification in a slightly different way than do the industrial groupings of the 1968 input-output tables. This is shown in the Appendix to chapter four. The data on employment are as in note 1.

(3) The ten product groups were:

Product Group 31	Pumps and Valves
Product Group 35	Mechanical Handling Equipment
Product Group 37	Industrial Plant
Product Group 38	Non Electrical Machinery
Product Group 39	Other Mechanical Engineering
Product Group 41	Scientific Instruments
Product Group 42	Electrical Machinery
Product Group 45	Radio and Radar
Product Group 57	Engineers Small Tools
Product Group 59	Hand Tools and Implements

(4) If the labour force in a given sector or sectors in general has more administrative, technical and clerical staff (ATCS) as a proportion of total employees in plants in more urban areas, and if these occupations are on average more highly paid than other grades (and this is not necessarily the case), then net output per head will rise in more urban areas, and labour productivity will need to be higher to maintain income

(or profit) from capital per head. However, across the fifty-four sectors, correlation of ATCS as a percentage of the total labour force with the percentage of the subregion defined as urban was significant in only one industry - Bricks and Fireclay.

(5) The minimum list headings are of the 1958 S.I.C.

6 Spatial patterns and variations

1 INTRODUCTION

This chapter describes the main variables used in the correlation and regression estimations which are considered in the following chapters. It looks predominantly at the magnitudes, spatial variations and product group differentials in the dominant variables. The chapter does not seek to explain but rather to describe these variations.

2 THE DEPENDENT VARIABLES

(a) Net output per head

For all product groups involved in manufacturing (i.e. 4 to 86) the average net output per head for the United Kingdom was £1,954 in 1968. The South East region recorded the highest net output per head of £2,153 and the Yorkshire and Humberside region the lowest at £1,791 per head, a regional variation of no more than 10% above or below the national average. By themselves however, these net output figures make no allowance for the different industrial mix of each region. A much larger differential in net output per head for the United Kingdom is however, to be found between the individual product groups studied, as shown in Figure 6.1. Product group 69 (Men's and boys' tailored outerwear) recorded a net output figure of £955 per head whilst at the top of range came product group 12 (Beer and malt) recording £3,645 per head, a range of between 86% above and 51% below the all industry national average. Of those product groups studied, thirty-five achieved net output per head figures below the all industry average and only eighteen product groups recorded figures above. Even after accounting for those product groups omitted from our analysis but represented in the total United Kingdom net output per head figures for product groups 4 to 86, there are still 25% fewer product groups operating at more than the all industry output per head than there are operating below it.

Figure 6.1 reveals considerable variation of net output per head across product groups, both within and outside SIC orders. The Drink, Tobacco and Chemical industries, all capital intensive sectors, have high net output per head values. The Engineering industry shows considerable stability in the performance of its product groups, twelve of the twenty-one product groups operating at net output of between £1,700 and £1,900 per head. The product groups within the Food manufacturing SIC order show the greatest variation of any order, whilst the Textiles, Footwear and Clothing industries, all labour intensive sectors, have consistently low values.

The pattern of net output per head across regions by product groups reveals a relatively high productivity performance in the South East region and poorer performances in the peripheral regions, especially Wales and, to a lesser extent, the South West and Northern region. In

Figure 6.1 Net output per head for each manufacturing product group in the U.K. used in the analysis in 1968

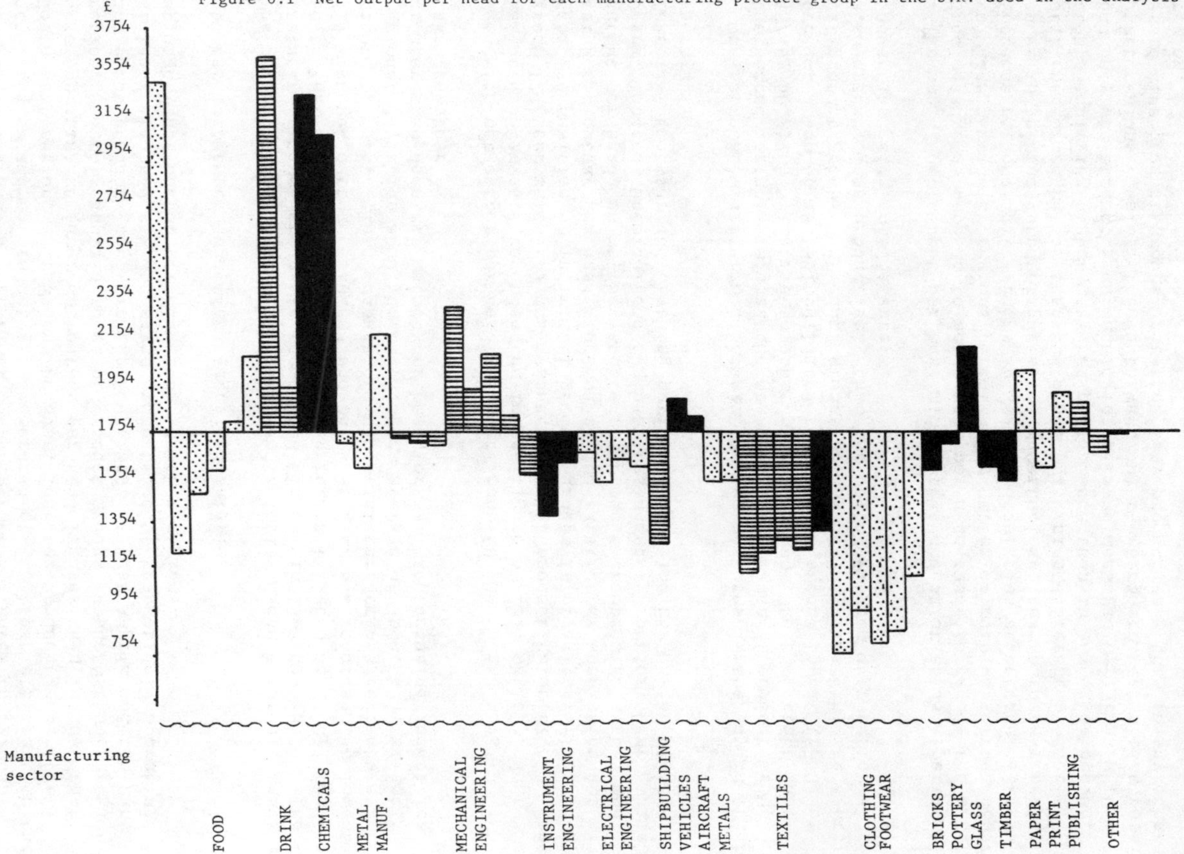

the South East region, fourteen of the fifty-one different product groups (26%) achieved higher net output per head figures than in any other region and no product group operated at its least efficient in the South East region. In Wales, however, fourteen product groups (26%) were operating at lower net output per head figures than in any other region, and this applied to eight product groups in the Northern region and eight product groups in the South West. East Anglia and the East Midlands also had six and seven product groups respectively operating at higher net output per head than in other regions.

(b) Net output per head minus wages and salaries

The net output per head minus wages and salaries measure for all manufacturing product groups in the United Kingdom in 1968 was £957. The South East region recorded the highest regional figure of £1,077 (as it did with net output per head) and the West Midlands recorded the lowest figure of £828. This measure of industrial performance reflects a regional deviation about United Kingdom average of about 13%, slightly greater than does net output per head for all manufacturing industries taken together.

As with net output per head, product group 69 (Men's and boys' tailored outerwear) recorded the lowest figure of £344 while product group 12 (Beer and malt) was measured as most productive at £2,552. The relative position of individual product groups is broadly similar, when using net output per head minus wages and salaries as when using net output per head, as may be expected. Product groups within the Food, Drink, Tobacco, Chemical and Engineering industries perform best, while Textiles, Footwear and Clothing perform well below the United Kingdom average.

One noticeable difference between the two measures is the way in which the second variable reduces the measured performance of product groups 48/49, 50, 52-55 relative to other product groups, to the extent that product group 48/49 (Shipbuilding) records the second lowest (£380) of all product groups. Product groups 50 and 52-55 in the Vehicles sector also operate less productively than the United Kingdom average for all industries using this measure.

The use of net output per head minus wages and salaries as a performance measure as opposed to net output per head tends to reduce the extent to which particular regions perform much better or much worse than others (because regional differences in wages and salaries accentuate differences in the net output figures). Nevertheless, the South East region still performed better than any other, with nine different product groups achieving higher measured performance than in any other region, and only one product group achieving a lower measured performance than other regions. Wales, the South West and the Northern region each possessed nine product groups operating less productively than in any other region.

(c) Index of efficiency

The derivation of this index ensures that all United Kingdom efficiency figures are unity for each product group and regional differences manifest themselves in an index figure higher or lower than the average (national) level of efficiency for each product group. The efficiency index has two major implications for the measurement of industrial performance relative to the use of net output per head and net output per head minus wages and salaries.

Firstly, it tends to reduce the amount of variation and performance between product groups, to the extent that differences between product groups are only marginally greater than difference between regions within product groups. To illustrate this point, the lowest efficiency index in any product group and any region is in product group 27 (Aluminium) in East Anglia which recorded an efficiency of 0.82, while the highest, 1.13, is in product group 61 (Yarns and Thread) and this occurred in East Anglia. The net output per head measure, however, recorded an absolute low of £719 in product group 69 (Men's tailored outerwear) in Wales and an absolute high of £5,070 in Beer and malt in Yorkshire and Humberside.

Secondly, the efficiency index emphasises the performance of the South East region in possessing 24 product groups which perform better there than in any other region. It also shows fourteen product groups in Wales and ten product groups in East Anglia performing less well in those regions than elsewhere in the United Kingdom.

3 THE DOMINANT INDEPENDENT VARIABLES

This section considers the dominant independent variables: those used in both the correlation and regression analysis of later chapters.

(a) Size of manufacturing establishment

The measure used to reflect the influence of internal economies of scale was net output per establishment. The variation in this measure by product group is shown in Figure 6.2. The United Kingdom average net output per establishment for all product groups (4-86) was £167,000 in 1968. The highest figure (£1,347,000) was achieved in product group 52-55 (Aircraft industry). Other product groups recording high levels of net output per establishment were product group 12 (Beer and malt) (£765,000), product group 23 (Synthetic resins)(£636,000) and product group 81 (Paper and board) (£628,000).

The lowest net output per establishment figure was in product group 71 (Dresses and lingerie) (£40,000) and in fact all the Clothing and Footwear groups recorded net output per establishment figures below the national all industry average. The second smallest net output per establishment figure was in product group 80 (Timber and wood manufacturers).

No clear spatial pattern emerges of average plant sizes, and there is no strong a priori reason to expect such a pattern, except perhaps on the basis of recent growth rates of new industrial sectors. The Northern region, Wales, Scotland and East Anglia for example have

Figure 6.2 Net output per establishment for each product group in the U.K. used in the analysis in 1968

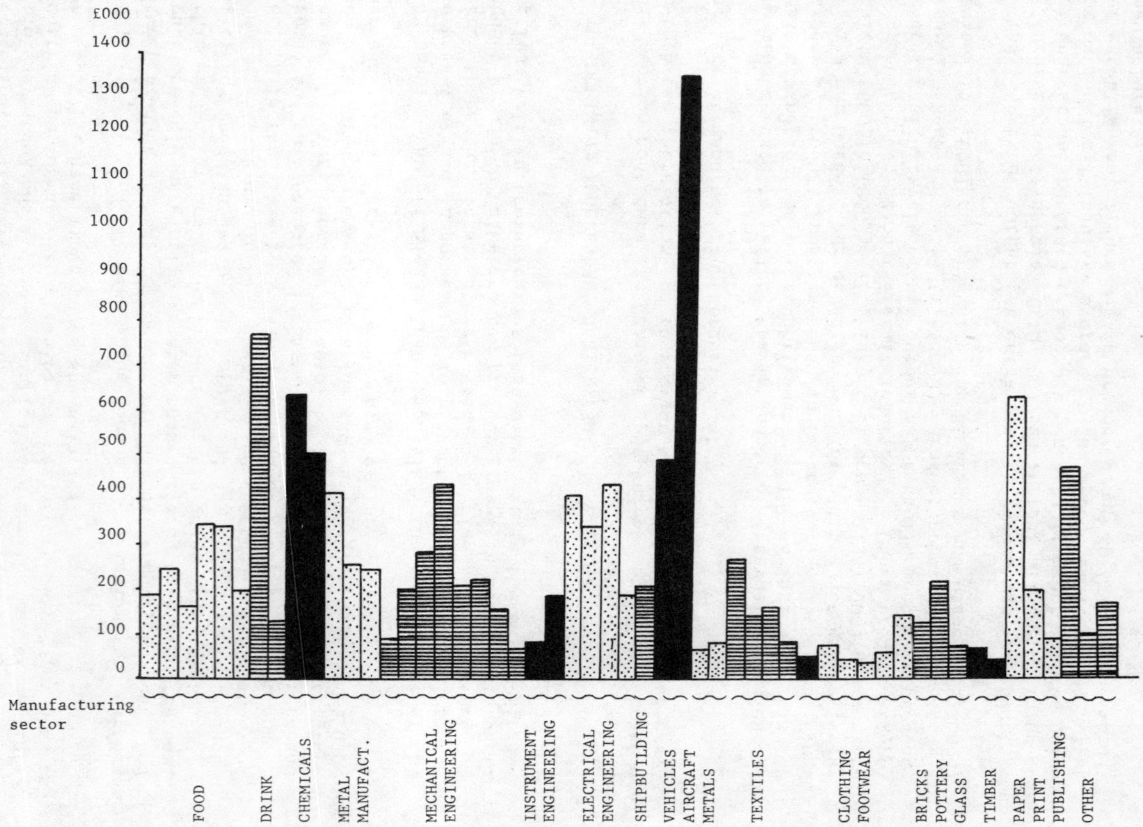

a higher incidence than other regions of product groups with average output per establishment values higher than in any other region. Overall, the distribution of both the largest and the smallest plants on average is fairly even across the regions. In the next chapter however we will find a strong correlation between this measure of plant size and the performance measures in many product groups when taken across subregions.

(b) Size of the manufacturing labour force

This variable was employed to measure the size of the labour pool and hence to give some indication of the availability of labour in each subregion. It also serves, however, as a more general economy of agglomeration measure being closely related to the size of each subregion and as such tends to correlate with other variables reflecting size such as population.

The subregional distribution of the manufacturing labour force is shown in Figure 6.3. The map shows the concentration of the larger labour pools in the conurbations and the more heavily urbanised areas. The influence of the way the subregional boundaries are drawn should be noted however. The non conurbation subregions of the West Midlands for example have large manufacturing labour forces. Other subregions which one might expect to be large on this basis are in fact smaller, as in South Wales or South Yorkshire or Humberside.

(c) Number of skilled manual workers

This variable also measures the size of the labour force in a subregion, but it was used to reflect an additional dimension of labour quality. It was used on its own in the regression equations and with other agglomeration proxies expressed as a proportion of the total manufacturing labour force.

The spatial distribution of this variable very closely follows that of the previous variable as might be expected. When expressed as a proportion, the variable had its highest values in subregions surrounding the largest urban areas rather than in the conurbations themselves. This is a cause and effect relationship with the metropolitan decentralisation of manufacturing plants in the post war period (Townroe, 1979, chapter three). The pattern of New Towns and Expanding Towns has contributed to this, especially in the South East and West Midlands regions.

(d) Employment in selected service industries

Eight different service industries were chosen as described in the last chapter, each in itself representing a different service used by most industries. Total numbers employed in the services were used as measures of the potential availability and use made of these services by manufacturing industry in each subregion. In this way each was expected to act as part surrogate for the economies of urbanisation. Within these service industries in 1968 there were a total of 1.97

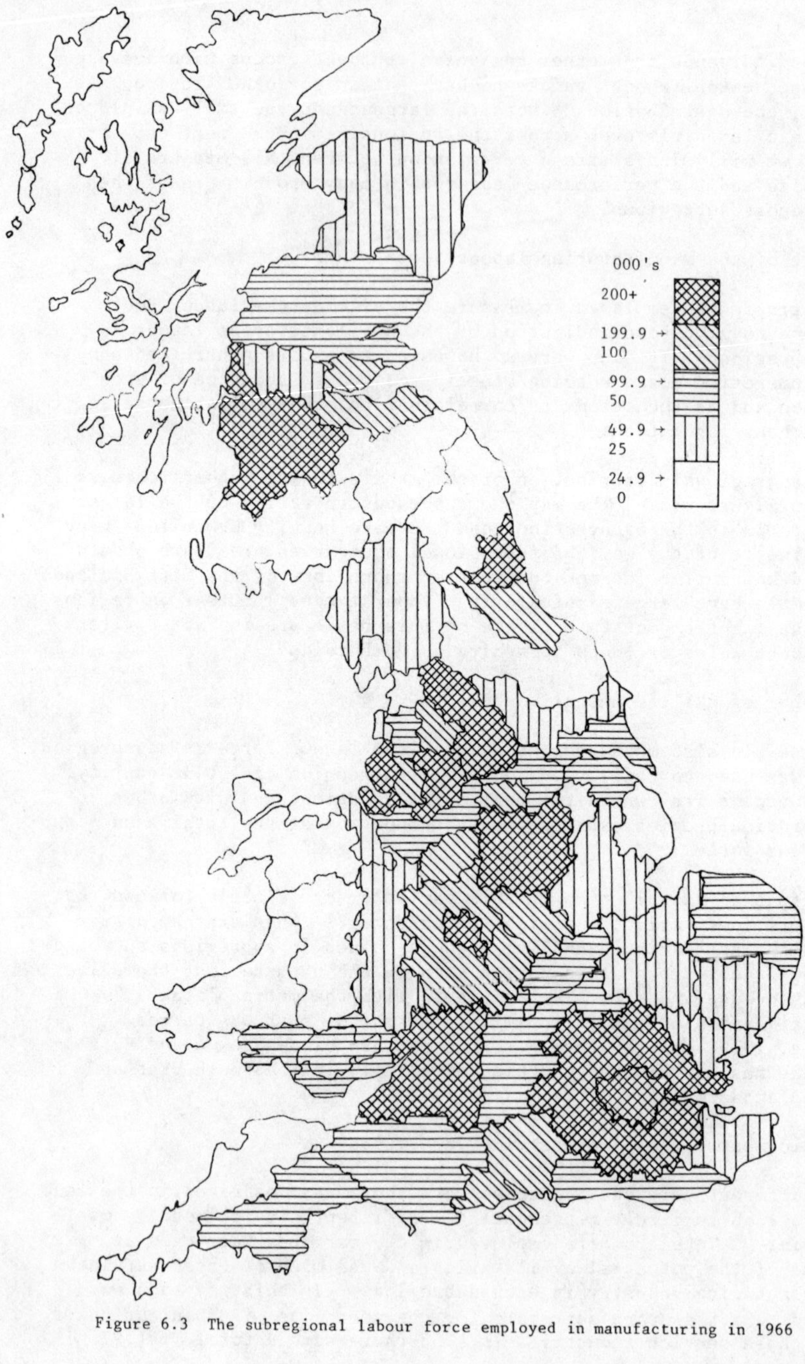

Figure 6.3 The subregional labour force employed in manufacturing in 1966

million employees of which one third was employed in Insurance, Banking and Commerce and one quarter in Wholesale Distribution. The smallest service industry chosen was Miscellaneous Transport Services and Storage with only 83,000 employees. Accounting Services and Legal Services employed just below and just above 100,000 respectively; Other Professional and Scientific Services nearly twice that. Road Haulage Contracting employed 240,000, and Dealing in Industrial Materials and Machines some 130,000. Across the regions the importance of these service industries in total and separately in 1968 varies considerably. This can be seen in Figure 6.4. Nearly half of the total service employment in Great Britain in these selected industries is employed in the South East region (978,000). The North West has the second largest number of service jobs in these particular industries whilst East Anglia and Wales record the smallest number, 42,000 and 57,000 respectively. The relative size of each service industry within a region is fairly consistent from one region to the next. Notable exceptions are the relatively small number employed in Road Haulage Contracting in the South East and the relatively large number employed in Wholesale Distribution in the North West.

Obviously enough, the largest absolute concentrations of these service jobs by subregion are in the conurbations and largest cities, and the smallest absolute concentrations are in the remoter rural areas. However, relatively, these jobs are more important in many of the rural regions, with the exception of the dominance of Greater London and parts of the Outer South East; particularly the rural subregions of Scotland, East Anglia and the South West.

Although the simple employment totals of these eight service industries taken together could have been used as a measure of potential agglomeration economies from the availability of these services, a first principal component (explaining 95.3% of the total variance) was calculated as being a better reflection of the pattern of these services across the subregions. The subregional scores were used as a variable. They are presented in Figure 6.5

This map shows up the strong presence of these service industries in the major conurbations. But it also shows the relative strength of the industries in many of the more rural subregions and the generally greater strength in the south of the country. The dominance of London however is absolute. All the factor scores lie between -1.03 and 2.14, with the two exceptions of the Outer Metropolitan Area (3.55) and Greater London (20.07).

(e) The rate of unemployment

As explained in the last chapter, this variable was initially introduced as a measure of labour availability. It is the average of the June and July rates between 1966 and 1970 in each subregion. However, when it was discovered that it correlated consistently negatively with each dependent variable, a rather different interpretation suggested itself. It seemed to be more a reflection of an older capital stock and of poor social infrastructures.

Figure 6.4: Employment in eight service industries by region in Great Britain in 1968

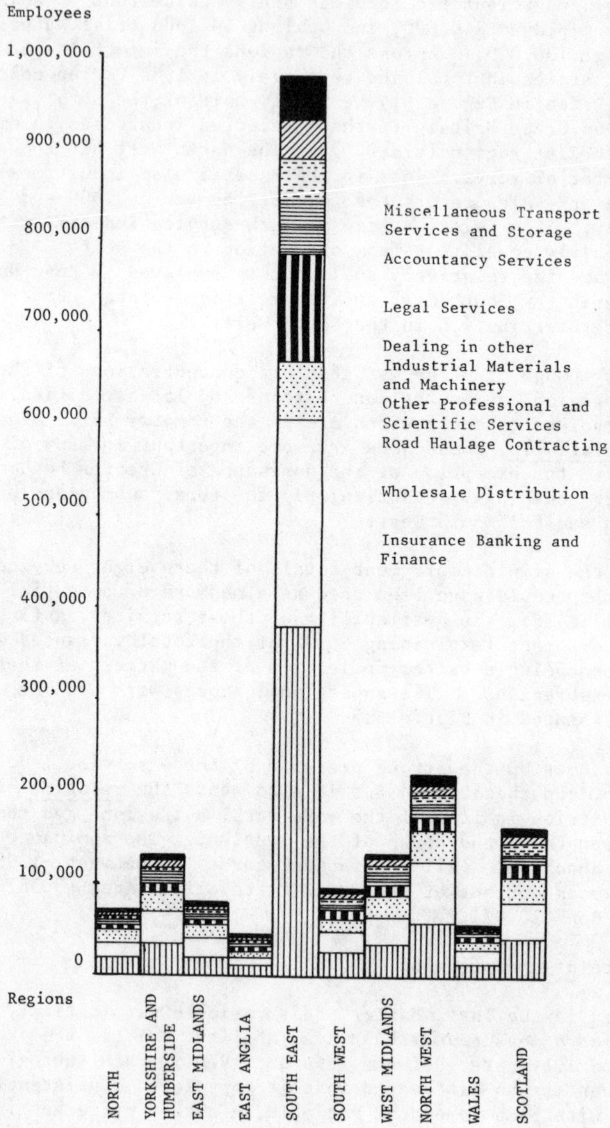

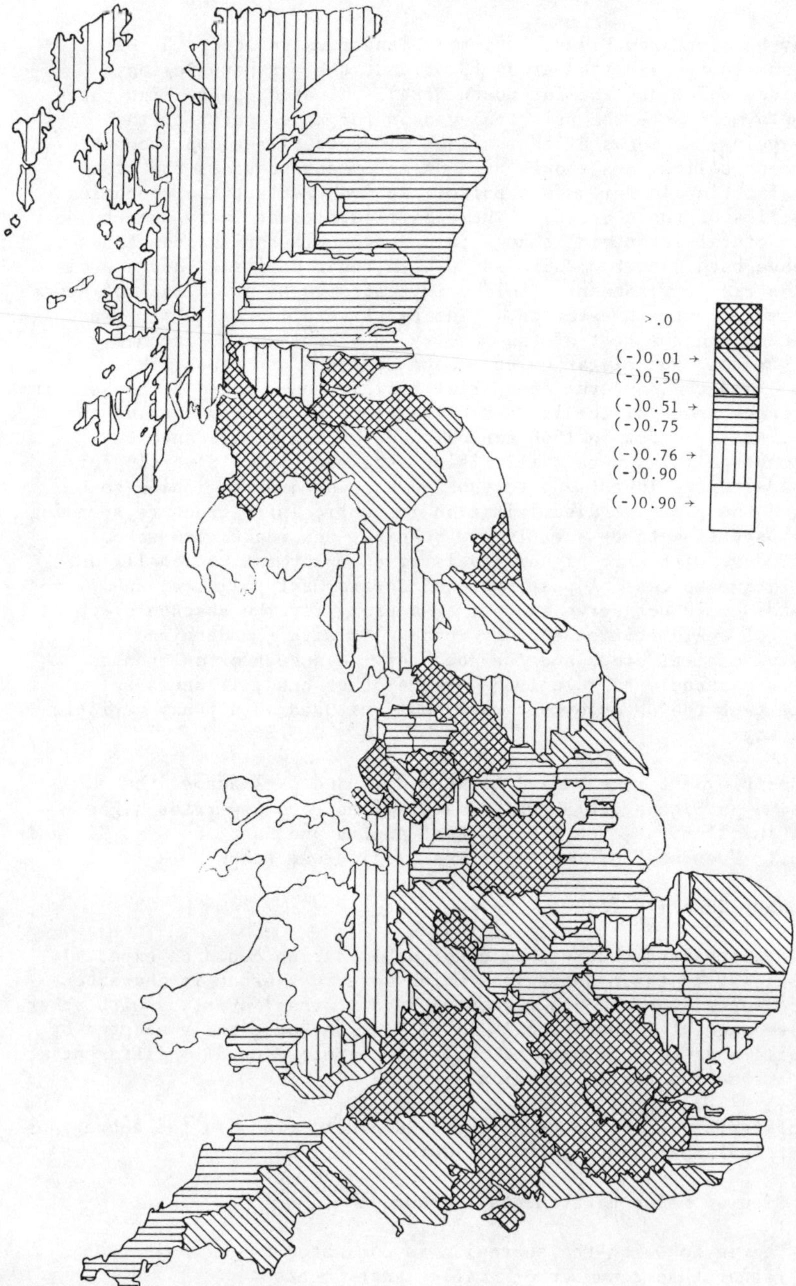

Figure 6.5: Subregional scores from a principal component of service employment 1968

As may be seen from Figure 6.6, the highest rates occur in the subregions in the Assisted Areas (Scotland, the Northern Region, Merseyside, Wales and the far South West). Indeed, these high rates of unemployment were the principal reason for those parts of the country being the focus of the various elements of regional economic development policy. Although high unemployment provides the strong political rationale for such a policy, it does reflect the economic difficulties of these areas. These difficulties are very much to do with structural industrial change in older manufacturing industries which have been slow to modify and update their capital; and a social and industrial environment of older infrastructures and a lack of new public and private investments. The relative differentials between these areas and the rest of the country in unemployment, incomes, activity rates, out migration etc. have lessened throughout the 1970's. And the concerns of spatial policies have moved to the problems of the inner areas of the largest cities both within and outside the Assisted Areas. But in 1968 expenditures on regional economic development policies were still rising, the successful diversion of new manufacturing investment to those areas was just beginning to be felt, and the positive discrimination in public infrastructure spending was only starting to be seen in new housing, new roads, new schools etc. Today, with much higher levels of unemployment nationally and with relative success of past regional development policies, unemployment rates would not serve as well as a proxy for the absence of that category of agglomeration economy which goes with a modernised responsive capital stock and the good service access of an updated social infrastructure. In 1968 on the other hand, it seems safe to argue that the unemployment rate could be used as a proxy variable in this way.

The unemployment rate varied between 0.7% and 5.6% across the subregions. As Figure 6.6 shows, no subregions recorded rates higher than 3% in all of the South East, East Anglia and East and West Midlands regions. Even most of the North West region was below this level.

(f) Urbanty/Rurality Index

It was hypothesised that economies of urbanisation could be expected to be largest in those subregions which were most urban in character and vice versa, even though the category of 'urban' overlaps with other variables used. A subregional classification, originally adopted by Fothergill and Gudgin (1979, p. 182) was therefore used to differentiate between urban and rural subregions.

The criteria used by Fothergill and Gudgin to classify the subregions took particular account of the following:

1 Size of major settlements in subregion

2 Degree to which the subregion is dominated by one major, rather than a number of smaller settlements

3 Function of the major settlement(s)

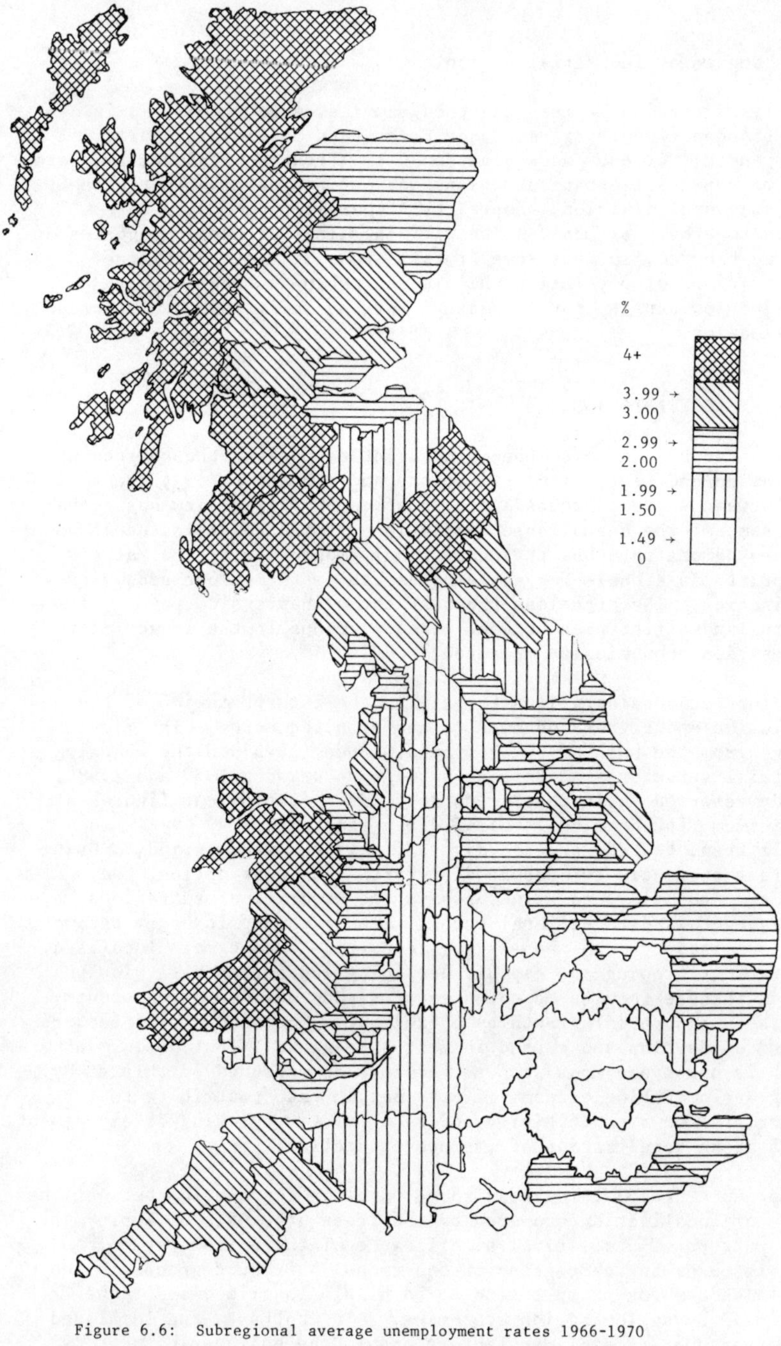

Figure 6.6: Subregional average unemployment rates 1966-1970

4 Degree of industrialisation.

This classification defined eight categories of subregion. Six of these (London, Conurbations, Major Free Standing Cities, Smaller Free Standing Cities, Industrial Non City, Urban Non Industrial) were taken to represent urban subregions for our purposes while the semi rural and rural divisions adopted by Fothergill and Gudgin were grouped together as rural. The dividing lines between categories of area are blurred, so that some 'rural' areas in fact have large concentrations of population while some 'urban' subregions have extensive low density rural areas. But the split is a useful crude approximation.

4 FURTHER CONTEXTS

This chapter has reviewed the main variables used in the subsequent correlation and regression estimations and has shown how these variables vary between product groups and over space. This review has emphasised some of the unavoidable limitations of the variables used, and the maps demonstrate how the subregional boundaries are not always appropriate as a basis for applying variables to measure economies of urbanisation. Nevertheless the next three chapters do reveal clear patterns and differences between product groups in the impact of the urbanisation economies as measured.

Two further considerations to take to the interpretation of the correlation and regression results can be noted here. The first follows from the work of Chisholm and Oeppen (1973) on the changing industrial structures of British subregions between 1959 and 1968, already referred to in chapter three. Using employment figures at the minimum list heading level of disaggregation, they found an overall trend towards greater diversification in the period. Using the Tress statistic to measure dispersion and localisation, they found that unemployment structures in the majority of subregions were converging towards a national mean. Manufacturing industry became less localised, though the service industries became more localised. Both rapidly growing and rapidly declining industries were widely spread. These results do not suggest strong agglomeration economy effects on industrial growth by subregion. Most industrial sectors can and do develop and expand in most subregions. But employment growth is not synonymous with performance as measured in this study. Strong agglomeration economy effects may in fact contribute to a raising of labour productivity and so a relative slowing of employment growth or an acceleration of employment decline.

By product group, this study found no clear correlation between the degree of localisation measured by the Tress statistic on employment and a pattern of statistical significance of the agglomeration variables used in the regression equations. Product groups in the textile sector for example tend to be highly localised and to be influenced by agglomeration economies. In contrast, the localised product groups in metal manufacture and in the engineering sectors are not so influenced by agglomeration economies; while certain non localised product groups (e.g. 4, 9, 74, 78, 80, 82, 83) have scored well with the agglomeration variables.

The second consideration is the possible influence of the New Towns policy on the subregional pattern of industrial performance. Sant (1975) and Keeble (1976) provide evidence to suggest that the development of the New Towns and, to a lesser extent, the Expanding Towns has had a significant influence upon the spatial pattern of manufacturing change in the post war period. Sant, for example showed that the impact of New and Expanding Towns by subregion was the most highly correlated variable with the volume of movement, out of a set of seventeen different potential influences on movement. Keeble shows that the eight New Towns in the Outer Metropolitan Area of the South East attracted in a net increase of 51,000 manufacturing jobs between 1959 and 1966. In Scotland, five New Towns attracted up to 50,000 manufacturing jobs by 1975, and Telford and Redditch in the West Midlands received 350 firms employing 27,000 in 1975. New Towns have developed their manufacturing base mainly in modern growth industries such as electrical, mechanical engineering, and vehicles.

These concentrations of new industrial investments may be reflected in particularly high levels of net output per head in the relevant product groups in the subregions in which the New Towns are located. In terms of relative size and importance however, it is probably only the Outer Metropolitan Area in the South East that was strongly affected in this way. In that subregion, with its eight New Towns, in forty of fifty-two product groups for which there are figures the net output per head is above the United Kingdom average. In no other subregion containing a New Town did more than half of the product groups exceed the United Kingdom average net output per head. Even if the New Towns in the Outer Metropolitan Area taken separately did product an upward bias in the subregional figure, it must be remembered that if there had been no New Town policy much of the industrial investment which went to the New Towns would still have taken place in the O.M.A. as part of a market induced dispersal from Greater London.

7 The key correlations

1 INTRODUCTION

Prior to the specification and estimation of a series of regression equations (reported in the next two chapters), simple correlations were employed to identify the dominant influences on the performance variables. Correlation coefficients were also used to identify statistical associations between independent variables.

This chapter looks first at the importance of internal economies of scale and the variables used to measure these effects. It then considers the importance of external economies of scale through different groups of variables (i) labour force variables, (ii) service employment total variables (iii) service employment change variables (iv) size of agglomeration variables (v) characteristics of subregion variables. Finally the chapter briefly considers those product groups which fail to achieve significant correlation coefficients with any of the variables. The chapter identifies those variables which appear to perform well and will therefore be important in the regression analysis; those variables which are consistently insignificant and will therefore play no further part in the regression analysis; and those variables which are intercorrelated and are therefore likely to present multicollinearity in the regression estimations should they all be included.

2 INTERNAL ECONOMIES OF SCALE

Three different size of plant variables were adopted: value of net output per establishment; the log of net output per establishment; and the average number of employees per establishment.

Table 7.1
Correlation coefficients for the potential size of plant variables for all manufacturing industry by subregion

	Size of plant variables	1	2	3
1	New output per establishment	1.000	0.959	0.942
2	Log net output per establishment	-	1.000	0.909
3	Average number employed per establishment	-	-	1.000

Table 7.1 shows that the three potential size of plant variables are highly intercorrelated, with coefficients which are all positive and

significant at the 1% level for all manufacturing industries together.

By sector, the number and size of significant correlation coefficients between the three size of plant variables and net output per head, and net output per head minus wages and salaries, respectively, are very similar. Taking the simple correlations with net output per head, the net output per establishment was significantly correlated at the 52% level for twenty-nine of the fifty-three product groups, and at the 18% level for twenty product groups as shown in Table 7.2.

Table 7.2
Significance of correlations by product group between net output per head and establishment by subregion

Significance level	Net output per establishment (X_1)	Size Log of net output per establishment (log X_1)
1%	4, 6, 9, 11, 14, 26, 28, 34, 35, 37, 38, 41, 63, 64, 68, 73, 79, 80, 82, 83	4, 6, 8, 9, 11, 14, 26, 28, 34, 35, 37, 38, 45* 50, 64, 67, 68, 73, 74, 79, 80, 82, 83, 85
5%	5, 8, 12, 50, 67, 78, 84, 85, 86	5, 12, 23, 25, 29, 40, 41, 63, 71, 78, 86
10%	30, 45,* 61, 70, 71, 81	30, 52155, 59, 61, 76, 84
Not significant	23, 25, 27, 29, 31, 39, 40, 42,* 46,* 47,* 48/49,* 52-55, 57, 59, 69, 72, 74, 76	27, 31, 39, 42, 46, 47, 48/49, 57, 69,* 70, 72,* 81

(* = negative coefficient)

All but five of the fifty-three product groups recorded positive correlation coefficients (product groups 42, 45, 46, 47, 48/49) and the number of significant correlations suggests the presence of internal economies of scale. The highest correlation coefficients were recorded in product groups 4, 6, 14, 28, 34, 35, 37, 73, 82, 83. The logarithmic transformation of net output per establishment increased the total number of significant correlation coefficients at the 5% level to 35, and at the 1% level to 24 (see Table 7.2). It also increased the absolute size of the correlation coefficient in thirty-three of the fifty-three product groups.

The average number employed per establishment was significantly correlated with net output per head at the 5% level with only nine product groups (4, 14, 26, 28, 35, 37, 80, 82, and 83). Many of these were the same product groups achieving high correlation coefficients using net output per establishment as an explanatory variable. It also recorded sixteen negative coefficients (all insignificant) with net output per head. Overall the average number of employees per establishment did not perform as well as net output per establishment, or its log transform. The latter produced the most significant correlations with net output per head, all of which were positive except in Radio and Radar, product group 45, which recorded a significant negative coefficient of =0.526.

The highest number of significant correlation coefficients between net output per head and the three alternative size of plant variables were recorded in the following SIC orders: Food Drink and Tobacco, Mechanical Engineering, Textiles, Timber, Printing Paper and Publishing, and Other Manufacturing. Those product groups where net output per head does not seem to be related to plant size whatever means is adopted were 27, 31, 39, 42, 46, 47, 48/49, 57, 69, 72.

The simple correlations between the plant size variables and net output per head minus wages and salaries, produced very similar correlation results to those with net output per head. This is obviously to be expected given the extent of intercorrelation between the two dependent variables.

Table 7.3

Significance of correlations by product group between net output per head minus wages and salaries and size of establishment (X_1 and log X_1) by subregion

Significance level	Net output per establishment (X_1)	Log of net output per establishment (log X_1)
1%	4, 5, 6, 11, 14, 28, 34, 35, 37, 38, 41, 63, 64, 68, 70, 79, 82, 83	4, 5, 6, 11, 14, 28, 34, 35, 37, 38, 41, 64, 68, 73, 74, 79, 82, 83, 85
5%	9, 12, 26, 61, 73, 78, 80, 84, 85	8, 9, 12, 23, 25, 26, 40, 57, 61, 63, 67, 70, 80, 86
10%	8, 48/49*, 81, 86	29, 45*, 71
Not significant	23, 25, 27, 29, 30, 31*, 39, 40, 45*, 46*, 47*, 50, 52-55, 57, 59, 67, 69, 71, 72, 74, 76	27, 30, 31, 39, 42, 46, 47, 48/49*, 50, 52-55, 59, 69*, 72, 76, 77, 81, 84

(* = negative coefficient)

The average number employed per establishment was correlated significantly with net output per head minus wages and salaries at the 5% level in only seven different product groups (4, 14, 28, 35, 45, 48/9, 82). This variable also recorded negative coefficients in no less than twenty product groups, two of which were significant (product group 45 Radio and Radar, product group 48/49 Shipbuilding and Repair).

Overall it is clear that internal economies of scale as measured are important in the majority of product groups and that the log of net output per establishment represents the most accurate measure of these economies. The statistical results obtained using this variable are generally higher using net output per head as the dependent variable rather than net output per head minus wages and salaries.

3 EXTERNAL ECONOMIES OF SCALE

Thirty-nine different independent variables were correlated with net output per head and net output per head minus wages and salaries to test for the existence of a number of different forms of external economy of scale. The variables used are described in chapter five. Each variable was correlated independently with the selected dependent performance variables.

It was found that some product groups obtained considerably more significant correlation coefficients at the 5% level than others, and that certain proxy variables for economies of agglomeration produced significant correlation coefficients with both dependent variables on many more occasions than others.

As a result of this exercise certain variables were dropped from the subsequent regression analysis because they consistently produced insignificant correlation coefficients. Some variables were also excluded because they were found to be measuring the same factors as other variables and all were therefore highly intercorrelated. It was found for example that many of the variables expressed in absolute numbers turned out to be little more than subregional size proxies. In addition some new independent variables were added to the analysis in an attempt to overcome the problem of unavoidably measuring the size of the subregion and thereby establish measures of the relative characteristics of each subregion. Other new independent variables were introduced when it was felt that they might measure an agglomeration effect which the correlation results suggested had not already been identified.

(i) Labour force variables

These were introduced to reflect differences between subregions in the availability and quality of the labour force. Such measures as the size of the labour force and the unemployment rate were used to reflect the availability of labour, whilst wage rates, activity rates and the numbers of skilled and semi skilled workers all help to describe the quality of the potential labour force. Theoretically at least, the larger the potential supply of labour and the greater the availability of skills, then the increased likelihood that industrial performance, particularly amongst the labour intensive industries, will be higher.

All of these variables are only capable of measuring economies of urbanisation; they are not industry specific. For this reason, an

Table 7.4
Correlation coefficients between independent labour force variables for the U.K. by subregion

	1	2	3	4	5	6	7	8	9	10	11	12
1. Total employees in manufacturing (XXXXX1)	1.00	-	-	-	-	-	-	-	-	-	-	-
2. Female activity rate (XXXXX5)	0.62	1.00	-	-	-	-	-	-	-	-	-	-
3. Male earnings (XXXXX6)	0.36	0.38	1.00	-	-	-	-	-	-	-	-	-
4. Female earnings (XXXXX7)	0.52	0.55	0.43	1.00	-	-	-	-	-	-	-	-
5. Number unemployed (XXXXX8)	0.71	0.53	0.28	0.39	1.00	-	-	-	-	-	-	-
6. Per cent unemployed (XXXXX9)	(-).25	(-).28	(-).29	(-).42	0.19	1.00	-	-	-	-	-	-
7. Per cent employed in assisted area (XXXX10)	(-).20	(-).25	(-).19	(-).27	0.01	0.46	1.00	-	-	-	-	-
8. Economically active males (ECACTM)	0.89	0.51	0.34	0.53	0.76	(-).27	(-).17	1.00	-	-	-	-
9. Economically active females (ECACTF)	0.89	0.53	0.32	0.53	0.76	(-).27	(-).17	0.99	1.00	-	-	-
10. Skilled manual workers (SKILMN)	0.91	0.56	0.37	0.55	0.79	(-).27	(-).17	0.99	0.98	1.00	-	-
11. Semi skilled workers (SEMSKL)	0.91	0.55	0.37	0.55	0.79	(-).25	(-).15	0.98	0.97	0.99	1.00	
12. Log of total employees in manufacturing (LXXXX1)	0.78	0.70	0.52	0.63	0.63	(-).33	(-).28	0.66	0.63	0.71	0.72	1.00

additional variable, the number of employees in the product group in the subregion was also introduced to reflect an economy of localisation. This variable was based on the employment data provided by Professor Michael Chisholm. The data had to be transformed from S.I.C. minimum list headings to product groups, according to the scheme shown in the Appendix to chapter four. The variable was prepared for a subgroup of product groups. In these groups it was correlated with the main dependent variables and it was also introduced into three of the regression models used. The variable consistently performed badly. This is perhaps somewhat surprising: the size of a given industrial sector did not reflect a pool of local external economies as expected. On the basis of these tests, the variable was dropped from the analysis. It possibly presents an area for further research.

The twelve other labour force variables were correlated each with each other and with the three performance variables for every product group in the manufacturing sector. Table 7.4 shows the high level of correlation between total employees in manufacturing, the number of unemployed, the number of economically active males, and females, and the number of skilled manual and semi skilled workers. These variables measure the size and character of the labour force, reflecting economies of urbanisation.

The correlations between these variables and net output per head and net output per head minus wages and salaries tend to product significant correlation coefficients at 5% in the same product groups and with coefficients of similar magnitudes, seen in Table 7.5.

The manufacturing sectors not represented are drink and tobacco, chemicals, metal manufacture, instrument and electrical engineering, timber and other manufacturing.

Product groups 8, 37, 59, 64, 74, and 83 consistently achieve significant coefficients. Of these product groups, cocoa, chocolate and confectionery product group 8; industrial plant product group 37; hosiery product group 64 have an average employment size greater than the United Kingdom average for all manufacturing product groups, and all except product group 8 have wages and salaries accounting for a higher proportion of net output than the average for all manufacturing product groups in the United Kingdom. It seems therefore that significant correlations are occurring in the more labour intensive industries, as might be expected.

The significant coefficients were positive in every case except one (number of employed with net output per head minus wages and salaries in product group 30) and were highest in newspapers product group 83. The significant coefficients were also higher in product groups with net output per head as the dependent variable. Of these seven labour force variables the number of unemployed produced the smallest number of significant correlation coefficients. It is of note, however, that these coefficients are positive, unlike the coefficients obtained from using unemployment rates which when significant at 5% were all negative. It seems therefore that the number of unemployed is acting

Table 7.5
Significant correlation coefficients between net output per head, net output per head minus wages and salaries, and labour force variables, by product group

Dependent variables / Independent variables	Product groups with significant coefficients of correlation at 5% level with: Net output per head	Net output per head minus wages & salaries
Total employees in manufacturing (XXXXX1)	4, 8, 37, 59, 64, 67, 70, 74, 83	4, 37, 64, 67, 83
Number of unemployed (XXXXX8)	4, 37, 74, 83	4, 30*, 37, 74, 83
Number of economically active males (ECACTM)	8, 37, 50, 59, 64, 70, 72, 74, 81, 83	8, 37, 59, 64, 74, 83
Number of economically active females (ECACTF)	8, 37, 50, 59, 64, 70, 72, 74, 81, 83	8, 37, 59, 64, 74, 83
Number of skilled manual workers (SKILMN)	8, 37, 50, 59, 64, 70, 74, 81, 83	8, 37, 59, 64, 74, 83
Number of semi skilled workers (SEMSKL)	8, 37, 50, 59, 64, 70, 74, 81, 83	8, 37, 59, 64, 74, 83
Log of total employees in manufacturing (LXXXX1)	4, 6, 8, 29, 37, 48/49, 64, 67, 74, 76, 83	4, 29, 37, 83

(* = negative coefficient)

as a labour force availability measure unlike the rate which is discussed in more detail later.

The numbers employed in manufacturing and the log transform of this variable (see Table 7.5) both produced a large number of positive coefficients. These variables might both be providing surrogate measures of potential labour availability and if treated as such are more successful than the number of unemployed workers. The number of economically active males and females and the number of skilled and semi skilled workforce could hardly be differentiated in their relative effects on performance. All are highly intercorrelated, and whilst the numbers of skilled and semi skilled are more measures of the character of the workforce than its availability per se, their difference could not be distinguished.

The significant coefficient at 5% for correlations between the industrial performance variables and the other labour force characteristic variables (female activity rate, male and female earnings, and % unemployed (overall and in assisted areas)) are more widely distributed across product groups than the variables so far discussed and are more varied in their signs. As Table 7.4 shows, this group of labour force variables are also less intercorrelated than the others.

Table 7.6
Significant correlation coefficients between net output per head, net output per head minus wages and salaries and labour force variables by product group

Dependent variables / Independent variables	Product groups with significant coefficients of correlation at 5% level with: Net output per head	Net output per head minus wages & salaries
Female activity rate (XXXXX5)	4, 6, 9, 37, 46*, 48/49, 76, 79, 83	4, 6, 9, 37, 46*, 76, 79, 83
Male earnings (XXXXX6)	28, 29, 35, 37, 39, 48/49, 74, 78, 79, 83	35, 37, 48/49, 74, 78, 83
Female earnings (XXXXX7)	4, 5, 8, 9, 12*, 23*, 26, 31, 37, 48/49, 50, 79, 81, 83	4, 5, 8, 9, 12*, 23*, 31, 37, 79, 81, 83
Per cent unemployed (XXXXX9)	8*, 26*, 31*, 39*, 48/49*, 50*, 52-55*, 68*, 78*, 79*, 82*, 83*	8*, 31*, 39*, 48/49*, 79*, 82*, 83*
Percentage employed in assisted area (XXXX10)	4*, 5*, 6*, 29*, 42*, 68*, 69*, 79*	29*, 31*, 42*, 52-55*, 68*, 69*, 72, 79*

(* = negative coefficient)

Table 7.6 shows that once again the number of significant correlation coefficients at 5% are greater with net output per head as the dependent variable. The product groups producing significant coefficients also vary considerably with the independent variable being adopted, as do the signs of these coefficients.

Female activity rate, female earnings and male earnings, tend to produce positive relationships with industrial performance and significant relationships in similar product groups ranging across most manufacturing sectors to the other set of labour force variables. The exception occurs in product groups in the textile clothing and footwear sectors, which are conspicuous by their absence in correlations with these three variables. In addition, the instrument and electrical engineering product groups again produce no significant correlations at 5%.

The female earnings variable produced the greatest number of significant coefficients of all the labour force variables. These were often in different product groups than those in which the male earnings variable achieved significant correlation coefficients (see Table 7.6). These variables could possibly be acting as a measure of labour quality, or alternatively they may simply represent the cause of higher net output through the effects of financial inducements. These two variables were not carried forward into the regression analysis despite their apparent success in the correlation exercise, because of their close connection with the dependent variable net output per head minus wages and salaries.

The unemployment rate produced unambiguously negative significant correlation coefficients at 5% in product groups representing all manufacturing sectors except drink, tobacco, chemicals and textiles (see Table 7.6). This suggests that the variable is failing to act like a measure of labour availability (unlike the number of unemployed). Rather, it could be acting more like a proxy for areas with a decaying industrial environment and hence older capital stock, the higher unemployment rates therefore being associated with lower levels of net output, with lower returns to capital.

(ii) Service employment variables

Service employment totals in eight selected service industries were used as variables to reflect the potential size and availability of these services for different manufacturing industries in each subregion. At the 5% level these variables produced positive significant correlations with dependent performance variables in a variety of product groups. No significant negative coefficients were recorded.

Table 7.7
Significant correlation coefficients between net output per head, net output per head minus wages and salaries and selected service employment totals by product group

Dependent variable / Independent variable (Employees in 1968)	Product groups with significant coefficients of correlation at 5% level with: Net output per head	Net output per head minus wages & salaries
Road Haulage Contracting (RDHAUL)	4, 8, 37, 50, 59, 64, 70, 74, 83	4, 37, 64, 74, 83
Miscellaneous Transport Services & Storage (MSTRAN)	4, 9, 37, 50, 64, 70, 72, 74, 81, 83	4, 37, 74, 81, 83
Wholesale Distribution (WHOLES)	4, 37, 50, 59, 64, 70, 72, 74, 81, 83	4, 37, 74, 83
Dealing in Other Industrial Materials & Machines (DEALMT)	4, 37, 34, 59, 64, 70, 72, 74, 81, 83	3, 37, 45, 74, 83
Insurance Banking and Finance (INSURN)	4, 37, 50, 59, 64, 70, 72, 74, 81, 83	4, 37, 69, 74, 81, 83
Accountancy Services (ACCOUN)	4, 37, 50, 59, 64, 70, 72, 74, 81, 83	4, 37, 45, 74, 83
Legal Services (LEGALS)	4, 37, 50, 59, 64, 70, 72, 74, 81, 83	4, 37, 45, 59, 74, 83
Other Professional & Scientific Services (PROFES)	4, 8, 35, 37, 50, 52-55, 59, 64, 70, 72, 74, 81, 82, 83	4, 8, 37, 45, 74, 82, 83

The table 7.7 shows that there are consistently more significant coefficients between the service employment variables and net output per head than with net output per head minus wages and salaries. With both dependent variables among the service totals, the number employed in Other Professional and Scientific Services correlates significantly most frequently. As a general rule, it seems that either all or none of the service employment/dependent variable correlation coefficients are significant with a particular product group. Those product groups which display significant correlation coefficients for at least seven of the service employment variables are as follows:

Product group	Dependent variable
4 Grain Milling	Both
37 Industrial Plant	Both
50 Motor Vehicles	Net output per head
59 Hand Tools and Implements	Net output per head
64 Hosiery	Net output per head
70 Women's Tailored Outerwear	Net output per head
72 Other Clothing	Net output per head
74 Bricks and Fireclay	Both
81 Paper and Board	Net output per head
83 Newspapers	Both

The highest correlation coefficients for these service employment variables were recorded for product group 37, Industrial Plant. The coefficients varied from 0.56 to 0.60 with net output per head, and 0.49 to 0.55 with net output per head minus wages and salaries as the dependent variables. The tendency for either all or none of these service employment variables to produce significant correlation coefficients with particular product groups reflects the extent of intercorrelation between these eight independent variables.

Table 7.8 demonstrates the degree of intercorrelation between the service employment variables and their principal component variable (explained in chapter six). The extent of the intercorrelation clearly demonstrated the need to introduce only one service employment variable at a time into the regression estimations.

The introduction of the service employment variables in terms of absolute employee numbers unavoidably meant that there was a tendency for size of subregion to be measured. As such these variables are highly correlated with population, the numbers fo skilled manual and semi skilled workers, the numbers economically active and the numbers unemployed. Those product groups which achieve a high number of significant correlation coefficients with the service employment variables tend also to be successful therefore with the other size variables above. In an attempt to overcome this problem, the proportion of workers in services to the total population was introduced into the analysis as a further agglomeration variable (see (v)).

Table 7.8
Correlation coefficients between selected service employment totals

	RDHAUL 1	MSTRAN 2	WHOLES 3	DEALMT 4	INSURN 5	ACCOUN 6	LEGALS 7	PROFES 8	PCOMPI 9
1. RDHAUL	1.00	-	-	-	-	-	-	-	-
2. MSTRAN	0.875	1.00	-	-	-	-	-	-	-
3. WHOLES	0.912	0.984	1.00	-	-	-	-	-	-
4. DEALMT	0.922	0.976	0.992	1.00	-	-	-	-	-
5. INSURN	0.876	0.990	0.989	0.983	1.00	-	-	-	-
6. ACCOUN	0.915	0.982	0.996	0.994	0.989	1.00	-	-	-
7. LEGALS	0.920	0.977	0.986	0.982	0.989	0.990	1.00	-	-
8. PROFES	0.874	0.879	0.883	0.890	0.903	0.887	0.921	1.00	
9. PCOMPI	0.934	-	0.992	0.992	0.989	0.994	0.995	0.926	1.00

(iii) Service employment change variables 1959-68

The ratios of the 1959 employment levels to the 1968 employment levels in eight selected service industries were used to correlate with the dependent performance variables in order to investigate the relationship between productivity in manufacturing and the growth or decline in the availability of potential business services for that manufacturing industry in each subregion.

The results of this exercise failed to provide a relationship on which it was possible to make many general assertions.

Table 7.9 shows that using alternative dependent performance variables does not alter the general pattern of significant correlation coefficients and also that the significant coefficients are negative on two out of every three occasions. The employment change in the Miscellaneous Transport Services and Storage and other Professional and Scientific Services produced mainly positive correlation coefficients with the dependent variables. The other changes such as in Insurance and Legal and Accounting Services and also Road Haulage Contracting and the two Distribution variables all tended to produce negative coefficients. A negative sign, of course, suggests that growth in service provision 1959-68 correlates positively with improvements in manufacturing performance. Thus all but two of the service employment change variables appear to be acting as proxies for agglomeration economies. The positive signs with PROFCH might be due to the reclassification of certain services between 1959-1968, out of the 'other professional' category and into more specific service sector professions. The positive signs on TRANCH are difficult to explain.

Most product groups achieved some significant correlations between the service employment change variables and the dependent performance variables. The Drink, Chemical and Metal Manufacturing sectors represented the only major exceptions. Overall the engineering industry had relatively more significant coefficients than other sectors. No one particular service or group of services appeared to be of special importance to the engineering industry - significant coefficients were spread throughout the eight services. In the Textile, Clothing, Paper and Publishing sectors however most significant correlation coefficients were produced with the Accountancy and Legal Service employment change variables. These coefficients were negative.

Because the regression models used were cross-sectional, these changes in service sector employment variables were not used in the regression analysis. The objective there was to reflect point in time subregional characteristics. The correlations reported here could however be explored further as one reflection of changing patterns in agglomeration economies.

(iv) Size of agglomeration variables

A number of size variables were included in the analysis, acting as proxies for a variety of potential economies of agglomeration

Table 7.9
Significant correlation coefficients between net output per head, net output per head minus wages and salaries and service employment change variables, by product group

Dependent variable / Independent variable (Ratio of 1959:1968 employment)	Product groups with significant coefficients of correlation at 5% level with: Net output per head	Net output per head minus wages & salaries
Road Haulage Contracting (ROADCH)	4, 30*, 41*, 76, 82*	4, 30*, 41*, 72*
Miscellaneous Transport Services and Storage (TRANCH)	28, 39, 47, 69, 82	28, 39, 45, 82
Wholesale Distribution (WHOLCH)	5*, 11, 29*, 38*, 40, 46*, 48/49*	11, 29*, 40, 46*, 48/49*, 52-55*, 61*, 79*
Dealing in other Industrial materials and machines (DEALCH)	4*, 31*, 34*, 38*, 45*, 46*, 86	4*, 31*, 34*, 38*, 45*, 46*, 86
Insurance, Banking and Finance (INSUCH)	8*, 30*, 31*, 38*, 39*, 46*, 48/49*, 79*	30*, 31*, 39*, 46*, 48/49*, 79*
Accountancy Services (ACCOCH)	29*, 30*, 38*, 50*, 64*, 69*, 81*, 83*	30*, 40, 55*, 64*, 69*, 76, 78*, 81*, 83*
Legal Services (LEGLCH)	4*, 29*, 37*, 41, 46*, 48/49*, 50*, 61*, 64*, 69*, 70*, 75*, 81*	4*, 37*, 41, 45*, 46*, 48/49*, 50*, 61*, 64*, 69*, 81*
Professional and other Scientific Services (PROFCH)	6, 9, 11, 31, 35*, 57, 69	6, 9, 11, 31, 35*, 69

(* = negative coefficient)

which might accrue to manufacturing industry operating in large urban concentrations. Table 7.10 shows that the size of agglomeration population orientated variables produced significant correlations in many of the same product groups as the variables already considered reflecting urban size, notably product groups 4, 37, 59, 64, 74, 83. Coefficients which are significant are mainly positive suggesting few diseconomies of agglomeration measured in this way.

Of the four population related size variables, total population and its log transform produce the most significant coefficients. Urban population density performed badly, against expectations. These population variables were not used in the regression estimations however because of the extent of their intercorrelation with the labour

Table 7.10
Significant correlation coefficients between net output per head, net output per head minus wages and salaries and urban size variables by product group

Dependent variables / Independent variables	Product groups with significant correlation coefficient at 5% between size of agglomeration variables and: Net output per head	Net output per head minus wages & salaries
Urban Population Density (XXXXX2)	29, 37, 39, 83	29
Size of Subregion (XXXXX4)	6*, 8, 47, 59, 71, 78*, 82	6*, 8, 47, 59, 71, 78*, 81*, 82
Log Urban Population Density (LNXXX2)	39, 48/49, 76, 83	46*, 76, 80*, 83
Population (POPULN)	4, 37, 50, 59, 64, 70, 72, 74, 81, 83	4, 37, 59, 64, 74, 83
Log of Population (LNPOPN)	4, 14, 37, 48/49, 50, 59, 64, 72, 74, 81, 83	4, 29*, 37, 59, 64, 74, 83

(* = negative coefficient)

force variables which also tend to be very size dominated.

(v) Characteristics of subregion variables

A number of different variables were introduced in an attempt to measure further characteristics of each subregion. Three of these, URBRUR - an urban rural code, XXXXX3 - the proportion of the subregion classified as urban, and MIGRAT - the amount of net migration from the subregion, were introduced at the start of the correlation exercise.

Table 7.11
Significant correlation coefficients between performance variables and character of subregion variables by product group

Dependent variables / Independent variables	Product groups with significant correlation coefficients at 5% between the character variables and: Net output per head	Net output per head minus wages & salaries
Urban/Rural Index (URBRUR)	4*, 6*, 25, 37*, 48/49*, 76	4*, 6*, 25, 30, 37*, 57*, 80
Percentage of Subregion Classified as Urban (XXXXX3)	4, 6, 37, 64, 68*, 71*, 81, 83	4, 6, 30*, 37, 64, 71, 80*, 81, 83
Net Migration from Subregion (MIGRAT)	37*, 70*, 83*	37*, 83*

(* = negative coefficient)

Table 7.11 shows that the migration variable performed very weakly and was therefore excluded from further analysis. It was hoped that net migration might reflect the character of the area, high outmigration perhaps suggesting a lower quality of workforce.

The percentage of the subregion classified as urban fails to take account of urban development in rural districts adjoining major urban areas while use of the urban-rural index inevitably suffers from the problem of defining the interface inherent in this dual classification of subregions. Both measures however show that in product groups 80 and 30 (Timber and Machine Tools) net output per head minus wages and salaries is higher in rural areas. Other product groups which appear to perform more efficiently outside of urban areas with at least one of the two performance variables and one of the two urbanity measures are Chemicals (product group 25) Leather and Fur (product group 68) and Dresses and Lingerie (product group 71). These results should however be interpreted with considerable care because there are at least two good reasons why rural locations may appear to benefit industrial performance, which are not related to the external economy argument. Firstly, a high proportion of those plants operating in rural locations may have relocated and be using newer and more efficient machinery. Secondly, both net output measures of industrial performance include elements of rents and rates. These payments are likely to be lower in rural locations and as such are likely to raise the measured performance of rural manufacturers relative to that of their urban counterparts. Rates however only represent 1.5% of net output in 1968 for manufacturing industry in total in Great Britain and as such, are unlikely to introduce a large element of bias into the net output measures of performance. The proportion of rates in net output varied from 2.5% to 1.1 % in the Standard Orders of manufacturing industry.

Although the proportion of the subregion classified as urban achieved more significant correlation coefficients with the dependent performance variables than the urban/rural index, the latter was chosen for experimentation in the regression estimates, being less intercorrelated with other potential independent variables.

The results for URBRUR and XXXXX3, although showing a tendency in some product groups for a singificant urban-rural polarisation of industrial performance, do not record the same overall sharp urban-rural subregional contrast in performance measured in purely employment terms which Fothergill and Gudgin (1979) have recently highlighted. Perhaps this quite substantial difference in emphasis in the two sets of results points to the potential fallacy in seeing employment growth and industrial performance growth as virtually identical processes. Fothergill and Gudgin look explicitly at employment change but nevertheless talk in terms of the 'performance of firms' in what appears to be more general terms than just their employee numbers.

A further group of variables were constructed later in the correlation exercise, specifically for use in the regression models. A range of variables was expressed as proportions of the populations and employment totals of the subregions to overcome the dominance of a simple size effect. From those examined, two were carried forward: the manufacturing labour force proportional to the population (XX1POP), and the proportion of skilled workers in the manufacturing labour force (SKLXX1).

4 PRODUCT GROUPS WITH INSIGNIFICANT CORRELATION COEFFICIENTS

Thirteen product groups identified themselves during the correlation exercise as consistently failing to achieve positive or negative significant correlation coefficients between net output per head, net output per head minus wages and salaries and the extensive range of independent variables tested:

No significant coefficients at 5%

Product group 14 Soft Drinks and Cider
Product group 27 Aluminium
Product group 63 Woollen Products
Product group 84 Rubber Manufacturers
Product group 85 Lino Leathercloth

One significant coefficient at 5%

Product group 12 Beer Malt
Product group 23 Synthetic Resins
Product group 25 Other Chemicals
Product group 34 Construction Equipment
Product group 42 Electrical Machinery
Product group 57 Engineers Small Tools
Product group 73 Footwear
Product group 86 Other Manufacturers

These results would suggest that economies of agglomeration measured by the extensive range of variables chosen are of little importance to the net output per head of the industry groups listed above. These product groups are representative of many types of manufacturing industry but exclude the food, textile, clothing, bricks, potter, glass, timber, and the printing, paper and publishing sectors, the sectors in which evidence for the influence of agglomeration economies will be found in the regression estimations.

5 CONCLUSION

This chapter has summarised the results of the correlation exercise with a view to establishing the extent of intercorrelation between independent variables and high correlations between the dependent performance variables and the proxy variables available for measuring economies of agglomeration. It has also pointed to various product groups for which certain economies of agglomeration may be significant and provided some statistical justification for leaving certain intercorrelated variables out of the regression analyses which are considered in detail in the following two chapters.

8 The regression results by product groups

1 INTRODUCTION

This chapter and the next describe the approach used and the results of the most important part of the study: the regression analysis. A wide selection of regression equations were specified and estimated across sixty-one subregions during the course of the project. These were specified for three dependent performance variables (net output per head, net output per head minus wages and salaries, and the efficiency index) and an extensive list of independent variables all of which have been described in the earlier chapters. These chapters concentrate on describing and explaining the results of the final group of equations which were chosen on the basis of the results from earlier specification attempts applied to selected product groups. The results considered here apply to all fifty-three product groups. Firstly however this chapter explains the reasons behind the equations which were finally adopted and offers certain caveats which might be important in interpreting the results.

2 SPECIFICATION OF THE REGRESSION EQUATIONS

In specifying the regression equations it was the intention that, in total, the group of equations chosen should be able to test for the significance of a number of different influences on the performance of manufacturing industry over the fifty-three product groups and sixty-one subregions in Great Britain in 1968.

The independent variables chosen for use in the regression analysis were those which were expected to best measure (on both theoretical and statistical grounds) the effects of the following factors:

a) Plant/establishment related factors. This includes the effect of internal economies of scale measured by plant size.

b) Factors external to the individual plant/establishment. This includes economies of localisation, economies of urbanisation and any diseconomies of agglomeration that are present.

   Three different sources of urbanisation economy were investigated:

   (i) those general urbanisation economies for manufacturers resulting from differences in size and character of agglomerations in the subregions in which they operate,

   (ii) those urbanisation economies resulting from the presence of a labour force of a particular size and quality in any particular subregion;

(iii) and finally those urbanisation economies which accrue to manufacturing industry as a result of the availability of service industry in close proximity to the production processes.

In chapter seven, the strength of the relationship between a large number of different independent variables which could be used to measure the factors listed above, and the dependent performance variables was studied. In addition the extent of intercorrelation between many of the explanatory variables was also reviewed. As such certain independent variables were identified as being potentially better proxy variables and were utilised in the regression estimations.

Table 8.1 lists the independent variables by name and code and shows which factors they were intended to measure in the regression estimations. A number of different regression equations was estimated. A constant term was present in all the regression equations. This term however did not aid the interpretation of the hypotheses under investigation and is therefore only referred to in passing. It tended to be significant at 1% in all product groups with EFFINN as the dependent variables, but less significant with QQQQQQ and QQQQWS. One factor, the size of plant was forced into all equations because of its consistently high correlation coefficients with all the dependent variables. Other equations either tested one additional independent variable to study its impact in isolation, or incorporated a number of other independent variables to study the effect of a number of agglomeration proxy variables taken together upon the performance of manufacturing industry.

The expected signs on the regression coefficients of these variables were expected <u>a priori</u> to all be positive, except in the case of the second variable, the unemployment rate, and the seventh variable, the Urban-Rural dummy variable where the value of 1 was given to the rural subregions and a value of 0 to the remainder. Three different dependent variables were regressed upon ten different groups of independent variables, making in total a set of thirty different regression equations for estimation. These equations were as follows:

```
QQQQQQ )
QQQQWS (  =  f( LNNNQQ, LNXXXI) -------------------------- (1)
EFFINN )     f( LNNNQQ, SKILMN) -------------------------- (2)
             f( LNNNQQ, PCOMPI) -------------------------- (3)
             f( LNNNQQ, XXXXX9) -------------------------- (4)
             f( LNNNQQ, URBRUR) -------------------------- (5)
             f( LNNNQQ, XXIPOP) -------------------------- (6)
             f( LNNNQQ, SKLXXI) -------------------------- (7)
             f( LNNNQQ, PCOMPI, XXXXX9, URBRUR, LNXXXI)---- (8)
             f( LNNNQQ, PCOMPI, XXXXX9, URBRUR, XXIPOP)---- (9)
             f( LNNNQQ, PCOMPI, XXXXX9, URBRUR, SKILXI)--- (10)
```

Table 8.1
Independent variables used in regression estimations

Variable name	Variable code	Measure
Log of net output per establishment	LNNNQQ	Size of plant - internal economy
Unemployment rate average 1966-1970	XXXXX9	Proxy for the age of capital and social infrastructures in the subregion
Log of total manufacturing employees 1966	LNXXXI	Size of agglomeration in subregion and availability of labour
	SKILMN	Size of agglomeration in subregion and availability and character of labour force
Total manufacturing employees as a proportion of total population in the subregion	XXIPOP	Measure of relative size of labour availability in relation to overall size of the subregion
Total skilled manual employees as a proportion of all manufacturing employees	SKILXI	Measure of relative character of workforce and relative availability of skilled workers
Urban rural code	URBRUR	Character of subregion
Principal component of the number of employees in selected service industries in the subregion.	PCOMPI	Size of agglomeration and availability of potential services in the subregion

There are a number of reasons why one might expect the performance of different product groups (or industries) to respond very differently to the existence of different potential agglomeration economies and different combinations of agglomeration economy within the subregion in which they are producing. For example, a capital intensive industry which also happens to be very reliant upon the proximity of specific services might achieve very little improvement in its manufacturing performance resulting from the presence of a large and skilled labour force available for work. On the other hand, for a labour intensive industry, should the available labour have the required skills, this potential external economy of scale may have substantial and measurable consequences for the efficiency and productivity of that industry.

For reasons like these it could be argued that not only do different product groups require different equations to explain the effect of external economies of scale on performance but also that different equations should be specified for industries operating in rural subregions, urban subregions, development areas, non development areas etc. However, because of the limited number of observations for each product group (never more than sixty-one and twenty-two product groups with less than thirty observations) the same equations have been specified for each product group and for the whole of the United Kingdom taken together. The patterns of importance or relevance of particular equations for different product groups and different spatial areas of the United Kingdom have been considered by analysing the results of all equations applied across the board. In this respect the URBRUR variable is of considerable importance.

3 THE PATTERN OF RESULTS

The thirty different equations applied to each product group were analysed primarily with respect to the signs of the coefficients and the significance of the coefficients. The aim of the regression analysis was not to derive a high R^2 value at all costs by the introduction of step wise regression techniques and endless streams of derived and transformed variables applied in different combinations. Equally, interest was not in the predictive qualities of each equation and as such the actual size of each coefficient was only of little concern. The aim of the regression analysis was to test (i) the ability of individual variables to measure particular economies of agglomeration and (ii) to ascertain to what extent and in which direction (signs) these economies are significant in influencing the performance of different manufacturing product groups.

The results of estimating the ten equations are considered in three different ways:

(1) Firstly, the signs and the significance levels associated with each of the independent variables in each equation are described by product group. For this purpose product groups are grouped into broad sectors and the similarities and differences between the results of the different product groups within each sector are discussed.

(2) Secondly, the results from equations 1 to 7, are considered, independent variable by independent variable. In this way a clearer picture is built up of the way individual variables perform for all the different manufacturing product groups. It is shown that the performance of certain product groups and certain sectors is significantly related to some of these variables, and in other cases the variables appear to be quite unsuccessful in picking up the expected agglomeration effects which they were intended to measure.

(3) Thirdly, and finally, the results from equations 8, 9 and 10 are considered by independent variable; identifying the product groups for which the coefficients of these variables

are significant, the signs of these coefficients, and the ways in which the results differ between equations, and between the three dependent variables used.

These three approaches to the consideration of the results do not in any way pretend to be mutually exclusive. Rather, they were designed to overlap to a considerable extent in order to simplify the explanation of what amounts to a very extensive set of results and which, without careful presentation could seem to be both confusing and contradictory.

It is therefore suggested that each section can be taken in isolation, depending on the nature of the results in which the reader is interested, or, all three can equally be read together in which case the reader should accept our apologies for a certain amount of necessary duplication. The results from (2) and (3) above are presented in chapter nine.

It should be noted that the selection of agglomeration variables for use in the regression models does not entirely remove the problem of collinearity. In particular, PCOMPI and SKILMN have a correlation coefficient of 0.88, LNXXXI and SKILMN have a coefficient of 0.71, and URBRUR and LNXXXI have a coefficient of -0.67. The remaining coefficients are all much lower, but these three may influence the interpretation of the results.

4 DESCRIPTION OF REGRESSION RESULTS BY MANUFACTURING SECTOR AND PRODUCT GROUP

The tables in the Appendix to this chapter summarise the regression results in terms of the significance of the coefficients in equations 1-7 for each of the three dependent variables. The results for equations 8, 9 and 10 are summarised in the Appendix to chapter nine.

(a) Food (product groups 4, 5, 6, 8, 9 and 11)

In each of these product groups the signs and significance of each coefficient in equations 1 to 7 is similar using net output per head and net output per head minus wages and salaries as the dependent variable. The pattern changes more strongly when the Efficiency Index is used.

The size of plant variable (LNNNQQ) is always positive, generally significant for each product group and each equation at the 1% level and always significant at the 5% level.

The proxy variables for agglomeration economies achieve a certain degree of success in the food manufacturing sector with QQQQQQ and QQQQWS as the performance measures. Using equations 1 to 7, product group 6 (Bacon Meat and Fish) achieved no significant regression coefficients at the 10% level on the agglomeration proxy variables with either QQQQQQ or QQQQWS as the dependent variable. But with both dependent variables, product groups 4 (Grain Milling), 9 (Fruit and

Table 8.2
Product groups achieving regression coefficients which are significant at at least 10%, with QQQQQQ, QQQQWS, and EFFINN as dependent variables

Equation	Independent variable	QQQQQQ	QQQQWS	EFFINN
1	LNXXXI	4 8 9 11*	4 9 11*	4 6 8 9
2	SKILMN	4 8 9	4 8	6 8 9
3	PCOMPI	4 9	4	6
4	XXXXX9	4* 5*	4* 11	4* 5* 9* 11*
5	URBRUR	4* 9*	4* 9* 11	4*
6	XXIPOP	5* 9 11*	9 11*	9
7	SKLXXI	4* 9*	4* 9*	

(* = negative coefficient)

Vegetable Products) and 11 (Other Food Products) each achieved a number of significant coefficients at the 10% level, many of these however had negative signs, as shown in Table 8.2. Grain Milling achieved the most significant results, with LNXXXI and SKILMN being significantly different from zero and positive at 1%, PCOMPI being positive and significant at 5% and XXXXX9 and URBRUR having negative coefficients, significant at 5%. This industry is perhaps an unlikely candidate to exhibit a strong influence of agglomeration economies.

In equations 8, 9, and 10 a similar pattern emerged. Product group 4 achieved the greatest number of significant regression coefficients and variables XXXXX9 and URBRUR most frequently recorded significant coefficients, albeit at 10%. Coefficients on XXXXX9 were generally negative. PCOMPI was positive and significant for Grain Milling in equations 9 and 10 with both QQQQQQ and QQQQWS as dependent variables. This variable achieved no measure of success with the other food manufacturing product groups.

Overall the performance of the food manufacturing sector seems to be related more to the potential internal economies than to the externaleconomies available to the industry. Only in Grain Milling do external economies begin to have some significance and then, to a smaller extent than plant size.

The use of EFFINN as the dependent performance variable produces a large number of significant regression coefficients. The constant term and size of plant variables are positive and significant at the 1% level in the majority of equations and in all product groups except product group 5 (Bread Flour and Confectionery), and product group 11 (Other Food Products). In both of these product groups the constant is positive and significant at 1% but the size of plant variable is either significant and positive at 10% (product group 11) or negative and insignificant (product group 5).

The agglomeration proxy variables which achieve significant regression coefficients with EFFINN are also shown in Table 8.2. In the product groups other than 6(Bacon, Meat and Fish) fewer significant regression coefficients are obtained than when net output per head and net output per head minus wages and salaries are used as dependent variables. Product groups 4 and 9 still achieve significant coefficients with LNXXXI and XXXXX9. In equations 8, 9, and 10 XXXXX9 and URBRUR are most commonly significant, the former having a negative sign. XXXXX9 is highly significant and negative in product group 11.

(b) Drink and Tobacco (product groups 12 and 14)

This sector of manufacturing industry is represented by two drink manufacturing product groups: product group 12 (Beer and Malt) and product group 14 (Soft Drinks and Cider). Spirits and Tobacco (product groups 13 and 15) were omitted because of insufficient observations.

Both of the product groups used recorded significant and positive size of plant coefficients: at the 5% level in product group 12, and the 1% level in product group 14, in all equations 1 to 10, with both QQQQQQ and QQQQWS.

The agglomeration economy proxy variables were less significant for product group 12 than product group 14. In the former case LNXXXI and SKILMN recorded the only significant coefficients in equations 1 to 10, and in all cases these were negative.

In the Soft Drinks and Cider industry LNXXXI, SKILMN and PCOMPI were significant at 10% level and negative with QQQQWS. URBRUR was positive and significant at 5% with QQQQQQ and QQQQWS, suggesting the importance of a rural location for this industry.

The efficiency index, EFFINN failed to product significant regression coefficients with size of plant in the Beer and Malt industry. This is perhaps surprising. PCOMPI was significant at 5% and positive in equations 3, 8, 9, and 10.

Size of plant was positive and significant at the 1% level in product group 14 with EFFINN as the dependent variable. Again URBRUR showed its significance to this group in equations 8, 9 and 10, as did LNXXXI which was significant and positive in equations 1 and 8. XXIPOP was also positive and significant at 5% in equations 6 and 9.

The results in this sector vary considerably depending upon the product group and the dependent variable. Overall conclusions are difficult to draw however. It seems that product group 14 is best suited to a rural location and that positive agglomeration effects only manifest themselves if performance is measured by EFFINN. Then the size of the labour force, and the number of skilled workers seem to have some significance, as does the availability of services in the case of product group 12.

(c) Chemicals (product groups 23 and 25)

With both QQQQQQ and QQQQWS as the dependent performance variable, the size of plant variable produced significant regression coefficients with both product groups 23 (Synthetic Resins) and 25 (Other Chemicals) In the case of product group 23 these coefficients were positive and significant at 10% with QQQQWS and 5% with QQQQQQ, while in product group 25 the coefficients were positive and significantly different from zero at the 5% level.

Of the agglomeration economy proxy variables XXXXX9 produced negative significant coefficients in product group 25 and URBRUR positive significant coefficients. Overall however, evidence supporting the importance of agglomeration economies to the chemical industry did not present itself, as may be seen in the Appendix tables.

EFFINN as dependent variable achieved positive and significant regression coefficients at the 1% level on all size of plant in equations 1-10. External economies of scale were not significant, except for XXXXX7 for product group 25, and for URBRUR for product group 23 in an unexpectedly negative direction.

(d) Metal Manufacture (product groups 26, 27, 28)

Product group 27 (Aluminium) was conspicuous in the regression analysis because of its singular lack of significant coefficients in any equation with either QQQQQQ or QQQQWS as dependent variable.

In product groups 26 (Iron and Steel) and 28 (Copper and Brass) the plant size coefficient was positive and significant at 5% with QQQQWS and QQQQQQ. The agglomeration proxy variable coefficients were significant only with product group 26 with net output per head as the dependent variable. In all other cases the coefficients on the agglomeration proxy variables were insignificant, often with negative signs.

The Efficiency Index produced positive and significant regression coefficients with the size of plant variable in all metal manufacturing product groups. Product group 27 failed to produce any significant coefficients with the agglomeration proxy variables. However Iron and Steel produced significant 't' statistics with PCOMPI at 1% and SKILMN at 5%, and Copper and Brass produced significant 't' statistics at 1% with LNXXXI, 5% with SKILMN and XXIPOP, and 10% with PCOMPI. Of particular note was the success of equation 10 for product group 28 Copper and Brass, where all of the variable coefficients had 't' statistics significant at least at 10%.

Thus, it seems that with performance measured using net output per head, external economies of scale are of little importance for all but product group 26 in the Metal Manufacturing industry. The efficiency index however seems to provide a productivity measure which is influenced significantly by certain external economy proxy variables in product group 26 and product group 28. In product group 27 agglomeration economies appear to have absolutely no relationship to performance.

SOUTHAMPTON LIBRARY UNIVERSITY

(e) Mechanical Engineering (product groups 29, 30, 31, 34, 35, 37, 38, 39)

The Mechanical Engineering industry is represented here by eight different product groups. These are:

Product group 29 Agricultural Machinery
Product group 30 Machine Tools
Product group 31 Pumps and Valves
Product group 34 Construction Equipment
Product group 35 Mechanical Handling Equipment
Product group 37 Industrial Plant
Product group 38 Non Electrical Machinery
Product group 39 Other Mechanical Engineering

These product groups are very different in nature and as expected the regression results, when taken together for these eight groups, do not display any particular trend that might be applied to the Mechanical Engineering industry in general. Rather the results vary, firstly by product group, and secondly with the dependent variable which is the subject of the regression analysis.

Taking the regressions with QQQQQQ and QQQQWS as the dependent variables together those variables which achieve significant regression coefficients with QQQQWS tend also to achieve significant coefficients with QQQQQQ, sometimes with different signs but generally at higher levels of significance.

Product groups 30, 31, and 39 fail to record any significant size of plant coefficients at 10% with QQQQWS and at 5% with QQQQQQ in equations 1 to 7. These product groups obtained very few significant coefficients on the proxy agglomeration variables either with QQQQQQ or QQQQWS. Where significant coefficients were recorded LNXXXI and SKILMN (product group 30), XXXXX9 (product group 31, 39), the signs were negative.

Product groups 34, 35, and 38 each recorded coefficients on the size of plant variable which were significant and positive at the 1% level in equations 1 to 7, with QQQQQQ and QQQQWS. Of all the proxy variable coefficients for agglomeration economies in product groups 34, 35 and 38 with both net output performance measures in equations 1 to 7, only the URBRUR variable in product group 38 recorded significant coefficients at the 5% level. Product group 35 recorded PCOMPI, XXXXX9, and URBRUR significant at the 10% level with QQQQQQ as the dependent. Overall however, these three product groups, like product groups 30, 31 and 39, do not seem to be significantly influenced in their performance by external economies of scale. In equations 8, 9, and 10 many of the proxy variables for agglomeration economies have negative coefficients. XXXXX9 is negative and significant in product group 30, 31, and 39, and URBRUR is positive and significant in product group 30 and product group 38. Other proxy variables (except for size of plant) are insignificant.

Product group 29, Agricultural Machinery recorded a positive coefficient on the size of plant variable with QQQQQQ which was significant at 5% in equations 1 to 7. Otherwise however this product group recorded virtually no significant coefficients, even at 10% in equations 1 to 10. This suggests a complete lack of importance of external economies of scale and limited importance of internal economies to the production of agricultural machinery.

In contrast product group 37 Industrial Plant recorded highly significant and positive size of plant coefficients (at the 1% level) in all equations with both dependent variables. It also recorded significant regression coefficients for a number of the agglomeration proxy variables with both dependent variables. In particular SKILMN and PCOMPI were both very significant and PCOMPI is also significant at the 1% level in equations 8, 9 and 10.

It therefore appears that of all the product groups representing the Mechanical Engineering industry, only the performance of Industrial Plant manufacture seems to be influenced to any sizeable extent by agglomeration factors. In contrast internal economies of scale are highly significant in product groups 37, 34, 35 and 38.

If EFFINN is adopted as the dependent performance variable however, the significance of agglomeration economies to manufacturing performance in the Mechanical Engineering industry are increased. The coefficient on the size of plant variable is significant at the 1% level and positive in all but product groups 31, 35, and 39, where although positive the size of plant coefficients in the equations are insignificant even at 10%.

Three product groups, 29, 30 and 31 each record very few significant coefficients at the 10% level on the agglomeration proxy variables. It should be noted however that for product group 29 in equations 3, 9 and 10 PCOMPI is significant at the 5%, 5% and 10% levels respectively. Product groups 34, 35, 37, 38 and 39 show a greater response to the agglomeration variables, as seen in Table 8.3.

Table 8.3
Product groups recording significant regression coefficients in equations 1-7 with EFFINN as the dependent variable in the Mechanical Engineering industry

Independent variable	EFFINN - dependent variable		
	Significant at 10%	5%	1%
LNXXXI	38	37 39	34
SKILMN	29 35	37 38 39	34
PCOMPI	35	29 37 38 39	34
XXXXX9	31*		37*
URBRUR	35		
XXIPOP	35		
SKLXXI	35	39*	

(* = negative coefficient)

Table 8.3 shows how LNXXXI, SKILMN, and PCOMPI particularly, recorded significant coefficients in these product groups (remembering that these variables are somewhat collinear). In product group 34 each of these variable coefficients were significantly different from zero at the 1% level. Product groups 37, 38 and 39 also recorded highly significant coefficients. The significance of PCOMPI to performance measured by EFFINN was also reflected in equations 8, 9, and 10 in product groups 29, 34, 35, 38 and 39. All the coefficients in product group 38 were at the 10% level. XXXXX9 and PCOMPI did not record many significant coefficients in equations 8, 9 and 10 when applied for EFFINN to Mechanical Engineering product groups.

(f) Instrument Engineering (product groups 40 and 41)

This sector of industry is represented by product groups 40 (Photographic Equipment), and 41 (Scientific Instruments).

In equations 1 to 7 in which proxies for different economies of agglomeration were tested individually along with the size of plant variable, the latter was significant at 5% and positive for both product groups with net output per head and net output per head minus wages and salaries as the dependent variables. None of the equations produced significant coefficients at 10% for any agglomeration proxy variable. In the majority of cases the signs on these coefficients were negative.

In equations 8, 9 and 10 size of plant again showed itself as significant, but the agglomeration measures tended to product negative and insignificant coefficients in the regression equations.

With EFFINN as the dependent variable the results in product groups 40 and 41 were somewhat different. The size of plant variable was never significant at less than 10% and was generally negative for product group 41, Scientific Instruments. In equation 1 LNXXXI was positive and significant at the 10% level in product group 40, and at the 5% level in product group 41. XXXXX9 was negative and significant at 10% in the Photographic Industry in equations 4, 8 and 9, and product group 41 recorded a positive and significant coefficient on XXIPOP at the 5% level.

Generally this manufacturing sector is not greatly influenced by agglomeration factors. The significance of these factors does however vary with the performance measure adopted, and with EFFINN there is some evidence that agglomeration size and labour availability is of limited importance to product group 41 Scientific Instruments.

(g) Electrical Engineering (product groups 42, 45, 46, 47)

In product group 45 Radio and Radar, the size of plant regression coefficient was negative and significant at the 1% in equations 1 to 7. The other Electrical Engineering product groups achieved no significant plant size variables with either QQQQQQ or QQQQWS. The extent of significant coefficients on the proxy variables for external economies of scale was extremely limited for all Electrical Engineering product groups. Only in product group 46 Domestic Electrical Goods, were significant but negative coefficients derived at the 5% level for XXIPOP and SKLXXI, and in product group 47 Miscellaneous Electrical Goods at the 10% level for XXIPOP, again negative. No other significant coefficients were recorded in equations 1 to 7, with net output per head as the dependent variable. The apparent lack of importance of agglomeration economies was also suggested by the results obtained with QQQQWS as the dependent variable. The same external economy proxy variables attained the same level of significance as with QQQQQQ, but also included SKILMN and PCOMPI which recorded positive and significant coefficients at the 10% and 5% levels respectively in product group 45 Radio and Radar.

Equations 8, 9 and 10 only achieved any real measure of success in product group 46, where although individually the external economy proxy variables did not appear significant, when applied in combination they recorded highly significant coefficients. For example in equation 10 with net output per head as the dependent variable SKILXI, XXXXX9, and URBRUR, were all significant at 1% and PCOMPI at 10%.

With the exception of the effect in product group 46 of combining external economy proxy variables, the use of EFFINN as dependent variable served to further emphasise the insignificance of agglomeration economies to the performance of the Electrical Engineering industry. In regression equations 1 to 7 no significant regression coefficients for the agglomeration economy proxy variables occurred in either product groups 42, 45 or 46. In product group 47 SKILMN, PCOMPI and XXIPOP each obtained negative coefficients significant at only 10%.

It seems therefore that large plants act as a positive disadvantage for the performance of product group 45, whereas in general plant size is of little significance in the other three product groups. External economies of scale seem to be equally insignificant however performance is measured in the Electrical Engineering industry.

(h) Shipbuilding and Ship Repairing (product groups 48/49)

The size of plant coefficient in equations 1-10 was generally negative and insignificant with QQQQQQ and QQQQWS, and positive and significant at the 5% level in equations 1-7 with EFFINN. Many of the agglomeration economy proxy variables achieved significant coefficients, some with negative signs, with all three performance measures as shown in Table 8.4.

This table shows that although many of the variables recorded significant coefficients their signs are often different. For this reason it is difficult to draw any clear conclusions about the significance of agglomeration economies for the Shipbuilding and Repair industry. The age of capital proxy was however constantly negative, and significant, at least at the 10% level, whilst the signs on URBRUR reflect the urban locations of the Shipbuilding industry. With EFFINN as the performance measure, LNXXXI, SKILMN and PCOMPI were also positive and significant, suggesting again that external economies

Table 8.4
Significance of regression coefficients on each independent variable analysed for product groups 48/49

Agglomeration economy proxy variables	Dependent variables QQQQQQ	QQQQWS	EFFINN
LNXXXI	5%	(-)10%	5%
SKILMN	-	-	10%
PCOMPI	-	-	5%
XXXXX9	(-) 1%	(-) 5%	(-) 1%
URBRUR	(-) 1%	(-) 5%	-
XXIPOP	1%	(-) 5%	5%
SKLXXI	(-) 1%	(-) 1%	(-) 5%

might be of some benefit to the Shipbuilding industry. The results, using QQQQWS as the performance measure do not however endorse this conclusion. This measure however must reflect the poor profitability record of many of the larger British shipbuilders of the late sixties.

Equations 8, 9 and 10 only recorded significant results with EFFINN as the dependent variable. Equation 9 was particularly successful and has an R^2 of 0.695, size of plant positive and significant at 1%, and XXIPOP and PCOMPI singificant at 10%. URBRUR was however positive and significant in equations 8, 9, and 10, in contrast to the results in equation 5 with QQQQQQ and QQQQWS. The reason for this is not clear.

(i) Vehicles (product groups 50, 52/55)

This sector of manufacturing industry is represented by two quite different product groups: product group 50, Motor Vehicles, and product groups 52-55, Aero Engines. Not surprisingly the regression results for these two product groups are quite different.

In product group 50 the size of plant coefficient is insignificant when output per head minus wages and salaries is used to measure performance but is significant in all equations when EFFINN and QQQQQQ is adopted as the dependent variable.

Similarly with QQQQWS the proxy variables for agglomeration economies fail to record any significant coefficients in equations 1 to 10 for the Motor Vehicle industry. However with QQQQQQ, PCOMPI is positive and significant at 5% in equations 3, 9, and 10, and with EFFINN, SKILMN and PCOMPI are positive and significant at 1% in equations 2 and 3 respectively. In addition PCOMPI is also positive and significant at 1% in equations 9 and 10, and LNXXXI is positive and significant at 5% in equations 1 and 8.

The relatively poor showing of this product group is perhaps surprising given what we know about the extensive networks of suppliers to the motor vehicle assembly companies. Perhaps the answer is that these networks are increasingly nationwide (or even international) and local urbanisation economies are now of little importance.

In product groups 52-55 the size of plant in regression equations 1 to 10 only achieves significance at the 5% level with EFFINN as the dependent variable, and with each of the performance measures used as the dependent variable only XXXXX9 and URBRUR achieve any real level of significance: XXXXX9 at 1% with EFFINN and QQQQQQ, and 5% with QQQQWS, and URBRUR at 5% with QQQQQQ and QQQQWS. The sign on XXXXX9 is negative, suggesting that poor performance in the aircraft industry tends to be associated with locations in the old industrial conurbations, and the sign on URBRUR is positive suggesting that more rural locations accompany improved performance in this product group. The other agglomeration factors failed to achieve any level of significance.

(j) Other Metal Goods (product groups 57 and 59)

In this sector of manufacturing industry the regression results suggest that whichever way performance is measured (QQQQQQ, QQQQWS or EFFINN), the significance of external economies of scale is limited. In product group 57 only the coefficient on SKLXXI is significant with EFFINN and the sign is negative. In product group 59 SKILMN is significant at 5% and positive with all three dependent variables and PCOMPI with EFFINN and QQQQQQ. The coefficients on all other proxy agglomeration economy variables are insignificant. It should be noted however that the significance of PCOMPI in product group 59 is also manifest in equations 9 and 10 with EFFINN and QQQQQQ.

In both product groups the significance and sign of the size of plant coefficient varies depending on which measure of manufacturing performance is used. With QQQQQQ is it insignificant in product groups 57 and 59. With QQQQWS plant size is positive and significant at the 5% level in equations 1, 2, 3, 4, and 6 and 7 in product group 57 but insignificant in product group 59. In contrast, with the efficiency index used to measure productivity, internal economies of scale are significant at the 10% level in product group 57 and equations 1, 2, 3, 4, and 6 and 7, but act in a negative direction. In product group 59 the size of plant variable has a positive and significant coefficient at the 1% level in all equations 1 to 10. No clear pattern emerges.

(k) Textiles (product groups 61, 63, 64 and 67)

Four different product groups represent the Textile industry, product group 61 Yarns and Thread; product group 63 Woollen Products; product group 64 Hosiery; and product group 67 Textile Manufactures.

The significance of the plant size coefficient is variable with different performance measures. Using QQQQWS as the dependent variable the size of plant coefficient is positive and significant for all the textile product groups to the 10% level in equations 1 to 7. In product group 64 it is significant in equations 1 to 10 at the 1% level. With net output per head as the dependent variable the size of plant coefficient remains significant in product group 63 (5%), product group 64 (1%) and product group 67 (1%), but is only significant at 10% in equations 2, 3, 6 and 7 in product group 61. With EFFINN, the size of plant coefficient stays positive and significant at 1% in product group 67 and product group 64 but is insignificant in product group 61 and product group 63.

The significance of the coefficients on the proxy external economy variables varies with the product group within the textile sector but tends not to be affected greatly by the choice of dependent variable in the regression equation. As such product groups 61, 63 and 67 record no coefficients on the external economy proxy variables which are significant at 5% with any of the dependent variables, in equations 1 to 7. Only product group 64 is successful in producing significant coefficients on these variables. With QQQQWS, SKILMN and PCOMPI are both positive and significant at 5% in equations 2 and 3 respectively. With QQQQQQ, LNXXXI is positive and significant at 5% whilst SKILMN and PCOMPI increase in significance to the 1% level. With EFFINN, all three, LNXXXI, SKILMN, and PCOMPI are positive and significant at 1%, XXXXX9 is negative and significant at 5% and XXIPOP is positive and significant at the 5% level.

Thus the evidence from equations 1 to 7 suggests that, whilst as a whole agglomeration factors are not of great importance to the performance of the textile industry, in one group, Hosiery, there is significant benefit from agglomeration economies. Looking more closely at equations 8, 9, and 10, product group 64 recorded significant coefficients at 1% for its plant size variable with all the dependent variables, and many significant coefficients on the agglomeration economy proxy variables. In particular all four agglomeration economy variables achieve significant coefficients at 10% in equation 8 with EFFINN as the dependent variable. Equations 8, 9, and 10 also tend to stress the importance of PCOMPI to the performance of all product groups in the textile industry. This variable achieved a significant coefficient at least at 10% in eighteen of the thirty-six equations, (four product groups, three sets of dependent variables, three sets of independent variables). Equations 8, 9, and 10 performed most successfully with EFFINN as the dependent variable.

(1) Clothing (product groups 68, 69, 70, 71, 72, and 73)

There are six product groups representing the clothing industry in Great Britain: product group 68 Leather and Fur, product group 69 Men's Tailored Outerwear, product group 70 Women's Tailored Outerwear, product group 71 Dresses, Lingerie, product group 72 Other Clothing, and product group 73 Footwear.

With net output per head minus wages and salaries as the dependent performance variable, the size of plant variable affects performance positively and significantly in product group 70 at the 5% level, in product groups 68 and 73 at the 1% level, and in product group 71 at the 10% level. In product groups 69 and 72 internal economies do not appear to be significantly related to QQQQWS. Equally in product groups 69, 71 and 72 the variables introduced to measure external economies of scale achieve no significant results, again perhaps reflecting low profitability levels masking agglomeration effects.

In product group 68 however the age of capital proxy XXXXX9 was negative and significant at the 1% level in equation 4, and also highly significant in equations 8, 9 and 10. In no other product groups was XXXXX9 significant with QQQQWS. In product group 70, all agglomeration proxy variables in equations 1 to 7 achieved significant coefficients at the 10% level except XXXXX9. Product group 73 had SKILMN positive and significant at 5% and URBRUR positive and significant at 10% In equations 8, 9 and 10 in product group 73 the agglomeration factors tended to work better in combination than they had individually in equations 1 to 7. In equation 10 for example PCOMPI, XXXXX9 and URBRUR were all significant at 10% or better. The same was also true in product group 71 where in equation 10 SKILXI, XXXXX9, and URBRUR were significant at least at 10%.

With net output per head as the dependent variable the picture changes somewhat with regression coefficients achieving higher levels of significance. Size of plant variables were significant in equations 1 to 7 in product groups 68, 71 and 73, and the significance of the agglomeration economy variables are set out in the table below.

Table 8.5
Significance of independent variable regression coefficients in product groups 68-73 with net output per head measuring performance

Product group	LNXXXI	SKILMN	PCOMPI	XXXXX9	URBRUR	XXIPOP	SKLXXI
68	-	-	-	(-) 1%	10%	-	-
69	-	-	10%	-	10%	-	-
70	5%	1%	1%	-	-	-	-
71	-	-	10%	(-)10%	-	-	-
72	-	(-)10%	5%	-	-	-	-
73	-	5%	5%	-	-	-	-

PCOMPI proves to be significant and positive for five of the six product groups in the clothing industry, and seems to be the most important proxy variable. In no other sector of manufacturing industry with QQQQQQ as the dependent performance variable does PCOMPI assume this consistent level of significance within a sector's product groups. The significance of the other external economy proxy variables vary with the product group concerned. Product groups 70 and 73 seem to be influenced most.

With EFFINN as the dependent variable the size of plant coefficient is also positive and significant in product groups 68, 71 and 73. More agglomeration proxy variables are significant with the EFFINN used to measure performance, than either QQQQQQ or QQQQWS. Whilst PCOMPI retained its importance, SKILMN also recorded five significant coefficients (all positive) with EFFINN. These were in product groups 69 to 73. All six product groups recorded at least three variables with significant regression coefficients. Equations 8, 9 and 10 each recorded a considerable number of significant coefficients on the agglomeration proxy variables. Product group 71 was particularly successful. Thus, it seems that when performance is measured by EFFINN in the clothing industry agglomeration economies are of considerable importance.

(m) Bricks Pottery and Glass (product groups 74, 76 and 78)

Each of the product groups 74 Bricks and Fireclay, 76 Glass and 78 Other Building Materials, recorded different regression results with net output per head minus wages and salaries as the dependent variable. In product group 74, size of plant was always significant in equations 1 to 10, at never less than 5%. Of the agglomeration variables only SKILMN and PCOMPI were significant, each at 5% and both positive in equations 2 and 3. PCOMPI was also significant and positive in equations 8 and 9. In product groups 76 and 78 however, the size of plant variable in equations 1 to 10 is not significant at any more than 10% and is often not significant at all. Product group 76 has XXIPOP and SKLXXI significant at 5% the latter having a negative sign, and LNXXXI and XXXXX9 significant at 10%, the latter having a negative sign. Product group 78 has only XXIPOP significant and positive at 10% of all the agglomeration economy proxy variables.

With net output per head as the dependent variable product group 74, Bricks and Fireclay achieves plant size coefficients which are positive and significant at 1% in virtually all of the equations 1 to 10. In addition SKILMN and PCOMPI record significant coefficients at the 1% level which are also positive. LNXXXI and XXIPOP are significant at 10%, the latter having a negative sign.

Product group 76, Glass, achieves a significant coefficient on all the proxy agglomeration variables in equations 1 to 7. It is to be noted however that in combination the agglomeration economy variables in product group 76 perform less well as witnessed by the results to equations 8, 9 and 10. In product group 78, the external economy variables only achieve significance at the 10% level in XXXXX9, XXIPOP and SKLXXI in equations 1 to 7. This industry might have been expected to be more strongly influenced by agglomeration factors. Size of plant is positive and significant in the majority of cases at 5%.

The efficiency index used as the dependent performance measure in product groups 74 and 78 gives a size of plant variable which is positive and significant in equations 1 to 10. In product group 76 the internal economy proxy variable is only sometimes significant and then at only 10%. The significant coefficients on the agglomeration economy variables vary with product group. In product group 74 they occur in LNXXXI (10%), SKILMN (1%), PCOMPI (1%), XXXXX9 (negative 10%) and XXIPOP (negative 10%). In product group 76, as with QQQQQQ, all are significant with LNXXXI and SKILMN positive at 1% and SKLXXI negative at 1%. In product group 78 only XXXXX9 (negative), XXIPOP and SKLXXI (negative) are significant; at 1%, 5% and 1% respectively.

With EFFINN as the dependent variable, the large number of significant coefficients in product group 76, equations 1 to 7, were not manifest in combination in equations 8, 9 and 10. Rather, these equations recorded better regression coefficients in product group 78 where individually the agglomeration variables were less statistically significant than in product group 76. For example in equation 10 in product group 78, the size of plant, SKLXXI, XXXXX9, and URBRUR are all significant at the 1% level. In contrast, in equations 8, 9, and 10 in product groups 74 and 76 only PCOMPI showed consistently to be significantly different from zero.

These results are very mixed, both by product group and dependent variable. A few conclusions seem to emerge however. Individual agglomeration factors seem important determinants of performance in product groups 76, and 74, and to a much smaller extent in product group 78. In product group 78 however agglomeration factors in combination also seem to influence performance. Size of plant seems to be important in product groups 74 and 78 but not so in product group 76. These results go against the usual image of the glass industry as being dominated by large capital intensive self-contained plants.

(n) Timber (product groups 79 and 80)

In product group 80 (Timber and Wood Manufactures) the size of plant coefficient is positive and significant at 1% with all three dependent variables in equations 1 to 10. The significance of the agglomeration effects seems to vary with the performance measure chosen. With EFFINN, both SKILMN and PCOMPI are significant at 1% and positive. No other agglomeration factors record significant coefficients in equations 1 to 7. In equations 8, 9 and 10 however URBRUR is significant and positive at the 5% level along with PCOMPI. With both QQQQQQ and QQQQWS however PCOMPI only achieves a significant coefficient in equation 8 with net output per head measuring performance. The other independent agglomeration variables however tend to record similar significant coefficients, with both QQQQQQ and QQQQWS. With QQQQWS, XXXXX9, URBRUR and SKLXXI are positive and significant, whilst XXIPOP, LNXXXI, and SKILMN are negative and significant. Equations 8, 9, and 10 tend to produce few significant coefficients on the agglomeration factors, the most common being with XXXXX9 and URBRUR.

In product group 79 (Furniture and Bedding) the size of plant variable is very significant and positive with all three dependent variables. The individual agglomeration variables vary in their significance, depending upon the performance measure chosen. Using the efficiency index to measure performance, all the agglomeration variables except URBRUR and XXIPOP are significant in equations 1 to 7, and all but

XXXXX9 at the 1% level. LNXXXI, SKILMN, and PCOMPI are also positive in their sign. In equations 8, 9 and 10, XXXXX9 and PCOMPI tend to be the only significant agglomeration variables. XXXXX9 is also highly significant in equations 4, 8, 9, and 10 with both QQQQQQ and QQQQWS as the dependent variables. With QQQQWS the only other significant agglomeration economy proxy variables are XXIPOP and SKLXXI, the latter having a negative sign. More variables are significant with QQQQQQ however, all except URBRUR obtaining some level of significance at less than 10% and all except XXXXX9 and SKLXXI being positive.

Overall, in both of these industries agglomeration economies seem to be quite important determinants of performance.

(o) Paper Printing and Publishing (product groups 81, 82, and 83)

In the case of most product groups the regression results using EFFINN as the dependent variable are, statistically at least, somewhat better than when QQQQWS is used as the measure of industrial performance. The same is equally true with the product groups in the Paper, Printing and Publishing sector of manufacturing industry. The groups are product group 81 Paper and Board, product group 82 Paper Manufacture, and product group 83 Newspapers. The results of each product group are best treated individually because no general conclusions can be drawn.

In product group 81 only two variables achieve any level of significance at 5% or above with QQQQWS as the dependent variable. These are SKILMN and PCOMPI. With net output per head as the dependent variable the results are little different. PCOMPI is significant at 1%, and is also the only significant variable in equations 8, 9, and 10, and LNXXXI comes in as positive and significant at 5% along with SKILMN in equations 1 and 2 respectively. Using EFFINN to measure performance the same agglomeration variables (LNXXXI, SKILMN, PCOMPI) are all highly significant and positive, along with XXXXX9 which is also positive and significant at the 5% level. The size of plant variable is only significant on occasions, perhaps surprising for this industry.

In the Paper Manufacturing product group (product group 82) the size of the plant is always positive and significant at the 1% level in each equation 1 to 10, and with each performance variable. Agglomeration effects however tend to be fairly insignificant. With QQQQWS and QQQQQQ XXIPOP is significant but negative, and with QQQQQQ and EFFINN, PCOMPI is positive but significant at only 10%. SKILMN is also positive and significant at 10% with EFFINN. The remaining agglomeration variables in equations 1 to 7 are not significant with any of the performance variables. In equations 8, 9, and 10, PCOMPI is often significant with QQQQQQ and EFFINN, as is XXXXX9 with QQQQQQ and QQQQWS, and XXXXX9 has a negative sign as expected.

In product group 83 the size of plant is constantly positive and significant at least at 5% (all equations). In addition the same agglomeration effects are significant (although to different degrees) whatever the performance variable adopted. With EFFINN, LNXXXI is significant at 5% and positive, whilst SKILMN and PCOMPI are significant at 1% and positive. PCOMPI and URBRUR are also positive and significant in equations 8, 9, and 10. A similar pattern of significance is found with QQQQQQ. With QQQQWS, however, LNXXXI is significant at 10%, SKILMN at 5%, and PCOMPI at 1%. In addition XXXXX9 and SKLXXI are both negative and significant at 10%. Only PCOMPI of the agglomeration effects records significant regression coefficients in equations 8, 9 and 10. These results reflect the urban locations of the larger newspapers. This may however be an industry in which modern electronic technology is reducing the significance of both internal and external economies of scale.

(p) Other Manufacturing (product groups 84, 85, and 86)

The product groups in this sector of manufacturing industry comprise product group 84 Rubber Manufactures, product group 85 Lino and Leathercloth and product group 86 Other Manufactures.

In product group 84 the results of the regression analysis vary with the performance variable adopted. With net output per head minus wages and salaries virtually no significant regression coefficients were recorded. With QQQQQQ and EFFINN the size of plant coefficient tends to be significant and positive, at least at 10% in equations 1 to 7, and the coefficients on LNXXXI and SKILMN are both positive and significant with EFFINN, at the 1% and 5% levels respectively.

In product groups 85 and 86, the size of plant coefficients are positive and consistently significant at least at 5% with all three performance variables. Apart from negative and significant coefficients on XXXXX9 at 5% in product group 85 with both QQQQQQ and QQQQWS, the only agglomeration economy proxy variables to record significant regression coefficients occur in product group 86 when EFFINN is the dependent variable. In this case, positive significant coefficients were recorded on LNXXXI, and PCOMPI at 5% and on SKILMN and XXIPOP at 10%. XXXXX9 and SKLXXI were both negative and significant at 5%.

It seems therefore that generally these product groups are significantly influenced in their performance by internal economies of scale, but external economies are considerably more limited in their influence and indeed only achieve significance in product groups 84 and 86 when EFFINN is used to measure performance.

5 CONTRASTING SETS OF PRODUCT GROUPS

The results of the regression analysis described in this chapter have shown that one set of product groups can be defined which in their performance are significantly influenced by external economies of scale. These were product groups 4, 9, 34, 37, 48/9, 50, 52-55, 61, 64, 68, 70, 71, 72, 74, 76, 78, 79, 80, 81, 83, and 86.

Equally, another set of product groups were found consistently to be unaffected in their performance by agglomeration factors. These were product groups 5, 8, 11, 12, 23, 25, 27, 28, 29, 30, 31, 40, 41, 42, 45, 46, 47, 57, 59, 61, 63, 67, 82 and 85.

The spatial distributions of the subregions having the four highest net output per head figures for each of the product groups in each of these two sets were compared. The results showed a clear distinction between those subregions where the two different sets of product groups had the highest labour productivity.

It was found that those product groups which were influenced in their performance by agglomeration factors tended to produce higher net output per head figures in subregions which were concentrated in the Midlands and the South East. In industries less influenced by such economies the subregions accounting for the highest net output per head figures were widely distributed throughout Great Britain; and the Midlands and South East were found to no more house the productive industries than any other region. Over one third of the subregions with the highest or second highest scores in the first group were in the South East region, two thirds if the Midlands and the Central South West and North West East Anglia are included. Only half as many in the second group were in the South East.

Certain other spatial patterns in the net output per head of particular product groups suggest possible localisation and urbanisation economy influences on performance. For example, some product groups record high productivity in adjacent subregions. This could suggest the importance of economies of localisation as well as urbanisation, for example in product groups 64, 79 and 82, all within the set of product groups generally influenced by agglomeration effects. Product group 64 (Hosiery) has high net output in subregions particularly concentrated in the South East. High net output per head figures in product group 79 (Furniture and Bedding) are concentrated in subregions in the Midlands, while for product group 82 (Products of Paper) the Outer South East is important.

Spatial grouping of subregions also occurs where product groups perform well in net output per head terms and yet are not influenced by the agglomeration factors tested to any large extent. In particular product group 12 (Beer and Malt) performs particularly well in four subregions in close proximity in the Yorkshire area. Product groups 27 and 28 (Aluminium and Copper and Brass) are both apparently little influenced by urbanisation effects and yet each performs well in pockets of subregions in the North West region and in South Wales. In a similar way product group 45 (Radio and Radar) performs best in a group of subregions located in the South East region.

The incidence of individual product groups performing well in contiguous subregions was found to be greatest amongst the product groups not influenced by the agglomeration factors tested. This result is a little surprising, because it means that the product groups whose best performances were spread more widely over the United Kingdom, ended up in more subregional groups than the product groups where the best performances in net output terms were more concentrated overall. This could mean two things. Firstly, those product groups affected by agglomeration factors have best net output per head figures in a concentrated area because these areas will offer urbanisation economies generally to many of these product groups. Alternatively, the product groups less influenced by agglomeration factors have their best net output per head figures in closely grouped subregions in a number of cases, either because of the significance of localisation economies to these groups, or because the urbanisation variables used were an inadequate test, or because of non-spatial factors fortuitously yielding a spatial pattern.

Table 8A1

Significance of the regression coefficients in equations 1-7 for each agglomeration variable, with net output per head (QQQQQQ) as the dependent variable

	Independent agglomeration proxy variables						
Product group	LNXXXI	SKILMN	PCOMPI	XXXXX9	URBRUR	XXIPOP	SKLXXI
4 Grain Milling Products	***	***	**	(-)**	(-)**	-	(-)*
5 Bread, Flour, Confect.	-	-	-	(-)**	-	(-)*	-
6 Bacon Meat, Fish	-	-	-	-	-	-	-
8 Cocoa, Choc., Confect.	*	**	-	-	-	-	-
9 Fruit, Veg. Products	**	*	*	-	(-)*	***	(-)**
11 All Other Food Products	(-)**	-	-	-	**	(-)*	-
12 Beer and Malt	(-)*	-	-	-	-	-	-
14 Soft Drinks, Cider	(-)*	-	-	-	**	-	-
23 Synthetic Resins	-	-	-	-	-	-	-
25 Other Chemicals	-	-	-	-	-	-	-
26 Iron and Steel	*	**	**	(-)**	-	**	-
27 Aluminium	-	-	-	-	-	-	-
28 Copper, Brass	-	-	-	-	-	-	-
29 Agricultural Machinery	-	-	-	-	-	-	-
30 Machine Tools	-	-	-	-	**	-	-
31 Pumps, Valves	-	-	-	(-)***	-	-	-
34 Construction Equipment	-	-	-	-	-	-	-
35 Mechanical Handling Equip.	-	-	*	(-)*	*	-	-

Table 8A1 (continued)

Product group	Independent agglomeration proxy variables						
	LNXXXI	SKILMN	PCOMPI	XXXXX9	URBRUR	XXIPOP	SKLXXI
37 Industrial Plant	*	***	***	(-)**	(-)*	-	-
38 Non Electrical Machinery	-	-	-	-	**	-	-
39 Other Mech. Engineering	-	-	-	(-)**	-	-	-
40 Photographic Equipment	-	-	-	-	-	-	-
41 Scientific Instruments	-	-	-	-	-	-	-
42 Electrical Machinery	-	-	-	-	-	-	-
45 Radio, Radar	-	-	-	-	-	-	-
46 Domestic Elec. Goods	-	-	-	-	-	(-)**	**
47 Misc. Elec. Goods	-	-	-	-	-	(-)*	-
48) Shipbuilding and 49) Ship Repairing	**	-	-	(-)***	(-)***	***	(-)***
50 Motor Vehicles	-	*	**	-	-	-	-
52 to 55 Aero Engines, Air Cushion Vehicles	-	-	-	(-)***	**	-	-
57 Engineers Small Tools	-	-	-	-	-	-	-
59 Hand Tools & Implements	-	**	**	-	-	-	-
61 Yarns and Threads	-	-	-	-	-	-	-
63 Woollen Products	-	-	-	-	-	-	-
64 Hosiery	**	***	***	-	-	-	-
67 Textile Manufactures	-	-	-	-	-	-	-

Table 8A1 (continued)

Product group	Independent agglomeration proxy variables LNXXXI	SKILMN	PCOMPI	XXXXX9	URBRUR	XXIPOP	SKLXXI
68 Leather and Fur	-	-	-	(-)***	-	-	-
69 Men's Tailored Outerwear	-	-	*	-	*	-	-
70 Women's Tailored O'wear	**	***	***	-	-	-	-
71 Dresses, Lingerie	-	-	*	(-)*	-	-	-
72 Other Clothing	-	(-)*	**	-	-	-	-
73 Footwear	-	**	**	-	-	-	-
74 Bricks, Fireclay	*	***	***	-	-	(-)*	-
76 Glass	**	**	*	(-)**	(-)*	***	(-)***
78 Other Building Materials	-	-	-	(-)*	-	*	(-)*
79 Furniture, Bedding	*	*	*	(-)***	-	**	(-)**
80 Timber & Wood Manufs.	(-)***	-	-	**	***	(-)**	**
81 Paper & Board	**	**	***	-	-	-	-
82 Products Made of Paper	-	-	*	-	-	(-)**	-
83 Newspapers	**	***	***	(-)*	-	-	-
84 Rubber Manufactures	-	-	-	-	-	-	-
85 Lino, Leathercloth	-	-	-	(-)**	-	-	-
86 Other Manufactures	-	-	-	-	-	-	-

Key * = regression coefficient significantly different from zero at 10%
** = at 5%
*** = at 1%

Table 8A2

Significance of the regression coefficients in equations 1-7 for each agglomeration variable with net output per head minus wages and salaries (QQQQWS) as the dependent variable

	Independent agglomeration proxy variables						
Product group	LNXXXI	SKILMN	PCOMPI	XXXXX9	URBRUR	XXIPOP	SKLXXI
4 Grain Milling Products	***	***	**	(-)**	(-)**	-	(-)*
5 Bread, Flour, Confect.	-	-	-	-	-	-	-
6 Bacon, Meat, Fish	-	-	-	-	-	-	-
8 Cocoa, Choc., Confect.	-	**	-	-	-	-	-
9 Fruit, Veg. Products	*	-	-	-	(-)**	**	(-)**
11 All Other Food Products	(-)**	-	-	*	*	(-)*	-
12 Beer and Malt	(-)**	(-)*	-	-	-	-	-
14 Soft Drinks, Cider	(-)**	(-)*	(-)*	-	**	-	-
23 Synthetic Resins	-	-	-	-	-	-	-
25 Other Chemicals	-	-	-	(-)*	**	-	-
26 Iron and Steel	-	-	-	(-)*	-	-	-
27 Aluminium	-	-	-	-	-	-	-
28 Copper, Brass	-	-	-	-	-	-	-
29 Agricultural Machinery	-	-	-	-	-	-	-
30 Machine Tools	(-)**	(-)*	-	-	**	-	-
31 Pumps, Valves	-	-	-	(-)***	-	-	-
34 Construction Equipment	-	-	-	-	-	-	-
35 Mechanical Handling Equip.	-	-	-	(-)*	-	-	-

Table 8A2 (continued)

Product group	Independent agglomeration proxy variables						
	LNXXI	SKILMN	PCOMPI	XXXXX9	URBRUR	XXIPOP	SKLXXI
37 Industrial Plant	-	**	***	(-)*	(-)*	-	-
38 Non Electrical Machinery	(-)*	-	-	-	**	-	-
39 Other Mech. Engineering	-	-	-	(-)***	-	-	-
40 Photographic Equipment	-	-	-	-	-	-	-
41 Scientific Instruments	-	-	-	-	-	-	-
42 Electrical Machinery	-	-	-	-	-	-	-
45 Radio, Radar	-	*	**	-	-	-	-
46 Domestic Elec. Goods	-	-	-	-	-	(-)**	**
47 Misc. Elec. Goods	-	-	-	-	-	(-)*	-
48) Shipbuilding and 49) Ship Repairing	*	-	-	(-)**	(-)**	**	(-)***
50 Motor Vehicles	-	-	-	-	-	-	-
52 to 55 Aero Engines, Air Cushion Vehicles	-	-	-	(-)**	**	-	-
57 Engineers Small Tools	-	-	-	-	-	-	-
59 Hand Tools & Implements	-	**	-	-	-	-	-
61 Yarns and Threads	-	-	-	-	-	-	-
63 Woollen Products	-	-	-	-	-	-	-
64 Hosiery	-	**	**	-	-	-	-
67 Textile Manufactures	-	-	-	-	-	-	-

Table 8A2 (continued)

Product group	Independent agglomeration proxy variables						
	LNXXXI	SKILMN	PCOMPI	XXXXX9	URBRUR	XXIPOP	SKLXXI
68 Leather and Fur	-	-	-	(-)***	-	-	-
69 Men's Tailored Outerwear	-	-	-	-	-	-	-
70 Women's Tailored O'wear	*	*	*	-	(-)*	*	*
71 Dresses, Lingerie	-	-	-	-	-	-	-
72 Other Clothing	-	-	-	-	-	-	-
73 Footwear	-	**	-	-	*	-	-
74 Bricks, Fireclay	-	**	**	-	-	-	-
76 Glass	*	-	-	(-)*	-	**	(-)**
78 Other Building Materials	-	-	-	-	-	*	-
79 Furniture, Bedding	-	-	-	(-)***	-	**	(-)*
80 Timber & Wood Manufs.	(-)***	(-)*	-	***	***	(-)**	***
81 Paper & Board	-	**	**	-	-	-	-
82 Products Made of Paper	-	-	-	-	-	(-)**	*
83 Newspapers	*	**	***	(-)*	-	-	(-)*
84 Rubber Manufactures	-	-	-	-	-	-	-
85 Lino, Leathercloth	-	-	-	(-)**	-	-	(-)*
86 Other Manufactures	-	-	-	-	-	-	-

Key * = regression coefficient significantly different from zero at 10%
** = at 5%
*** = at 1%

Table 8A3

Significance of the regression coefficients in equations 1-7 for each agglomeration variable with the efficiency index (EFFINN) as the dependent variable

Product group	Independent agglomeration proxy variables						
	LNXXI	SKILMN	PCOMPI	XXXXX9	URBRUR	XXIPOP	SKLXXI
4 Grain Milling Products	**	-	-	(-)*	(-)*	-	-
5 Bread, Flour, Confect.	-	-	-	(-)**	-	-	-
6 Bacon, Meat, Fish	***	***	***	-	-	-	-
8 Cocoa, Choc., Confect.	**	**	-	-	-	-	-
9 Fruit, Veg. Products	**	*	-	(-)**	-	*	-
11 All Other Food Products	-	-	-	(-)***	-	-	-
12 Beer and Malt	-	**	**	-	-	-	-
14 Soft Drinks, Cider	*	*	-	-	-	**	-
23 Synthetic Resins	-	-	-	-	(-)*	-	-
25 Other Chemicals	-	-	-	(-)*	-	-	-
26 Iron and Steel	-	**	***	(-)*	-	-	-
27 Aluminium	-	-	-	-	-	-	-
28 Copper, Brass	***	**	*	-	-	**	(-)***
29 Agricultural Machinery	-	*	**	-	-	-	-
30 Machine Tools	-	-	-	-	-	-	-
31 Pumps, Valves	-	-	-	(-)*	-	-	-
34 Construction Equipment	***	***	***	-	-	-	-
35 Mechanical Handling Equip.	-	*	*	-	*	*	*

Table 8A3 (continued)

Product group	Independent agglomeration proxy variables						
	LNXXXI	SKILMN	PCOMPI	XXXXX9	URBRUR	XXIPOP	SKLXXI
37 Industrial Plant	**	**	**	(-)***	-	-	-
38 Non Electrical Machinery	*	**	**	-	-	-	-
39 Other Mech. Engineering	**	**	**	-	-	-	(-)**
40 Photographic Equipment	*	-	-	(-)**	-	-	(-)*
41 Scientific Instruments	**	-	-	-	-	**	-
42 Electrical Machinery	-	-	-	-	-	-	-
45 Radio, Radar	-	-	-	-	-	-	-
46 Domestic Elec. Goods	-	-	-	-	-	-	-
47 Misc. Elec. Goods	-	*	*	-	-	(-)*	-
48) Shipbuilding and 49) Ship Repairing	**	*	**	(-)***	-	**	(-)**
50 Motor Vehicles	**	***	***	(-)*	-	-	-
52 to 55 Aero Engines, Air Cushion Vehicles	*	-	-	(-)***	-	-	(-)*
57 Engineers Small Tools	-	-	-	-	-	-	(-)**
59 Hand Tools & Implements	-	**	*	-	-	-	-
61 Yarns and Threads	-	-	-	-	(-)*	-	-
63 Woollen Products	-	-	-	(-)*	-	-	-
64 Hosiery	***	***	***	(-)**	-	**	-
67 Textile Manufactures	-	-	-	(-)*	-	-	-

Table 8A3 (continued)

Product group	Independent agglomeration proxy variables						
	LNXXXI	SKILMN	PCOMPI	XXXXX9	URBRUR	XXIPOP	SKLXXI
68 Leather and Fur	(-)*	-	-	(-)**	*	-	*
69 Men's Tailored Outerwear	-	**	**	-	**	-	-
70 Women's Tailored O'wear	-	***	***	-	*	-	-
71 Dresses, Lingerie	**	***	***	(-)**	-	-	-
72 Other Clothing	*	**	**	**	-	-	(-)*
73 Footwear	-	**	***	(-)*	-	-	-
74 Bricks, Fireclay	*	***	***	(-)*	-	(-)*	-
76 Glass	***	***	**	-	(-)**	**	(-)***
78 Other Building Materials	-	-	-	(-)***	-	**	(-)***
79 Furniture, Bedding	***	***	***	(-)**	-	-	(-)***
80 Timber & Wood Manufs.	-	***	***	-	-	-	-
81 Paper & Board	***	***	**	**	-	-	-
82 Products Made of Paper	-	*	*	-	-	-	-
83 Newspapers	**	***	***	-	*	-	-
84 Rubber Manufactures	***	*	-	-	(-)*	-	-
85 Lino, Leathercloth	-	*	-	-	-	-	-
86 Other Manufactures	**	*	**	(-)**	-	*	(-)**

Key * = regression coefficient significantly different from zero at 10%
** = at 5%
*** = at 1%

9 The regression results by agglomeration variable

The first part of this chapter looks at the success of each agglomeration economy proxy variable in turn, with respect to its significance for the performance of each manufacturing sector, whether performance is measured by net output per head, net output per head minus wages and salaries, or by the efficiency index. The second part considers the combinations of variables in equations 8 to 10.

1 THE AGGLOMERATION VARIABLES - EQUATIONS 1 TO 7

(a) Local services

The availability of selected services was measured by the first principal component taken from the numbers employed in the eight selected service sectors in each subregion.

Table 9.1
Product groups recording significant regressions coefficients on PCOMPI with QQQQQQ, QQQQWS and EFFINN as the dependent performance variables

Significant at	QQQQQQ	QQQQWS	EFFINN
1%	37, 64, 70, 74, 81, 83	37, 83	6, 26, 34, 50, 64, 70, 71, 73, 74, 79, 80, 83
5%	4, 26, 35, 50, 59, 72, 73	4, 45, 64, 74, 81	12, 29, 37, 38, 39, 48/49, 69, 72, 76, 81, 86
10%	9, 69, 71, 76, 79, 82	14*, 70	28, 35, 47, 59, 82

(* = negative coefficient)

Table 9.1 shows that the choice of performance measure has a considerable influence on whether the availability of services are significant to the performance of any particular product group. For example with the efficiency index measuring performance twenty-eight of the fifty-three product groups recorded a significant coefficient on PCOMPI at the 10% level or less. With QQQQWS however the total was only nine.

Only six different product groups (37, 64, 70, 74, 81 and 83) record a significant regression coefficient on PCOMPI with all three performance measures. Product groups 81 and 83 are both in the Paper Printing and Publishing sector of manufacturing industry. In product group 83

Newspapers the coefficient is always significantly different from zero at 1% whilst in product group 81 it is not greater than 5%. It seems therefore that service availability is a very important consideration for this particular sector of manufacturing.

The other four product groups are each representative of different industrial orders and in each one the coefficient is significant at the 1% level with at least two of the three performance measures, although not always the same two. In all six of these product groups therefore the availability of services seems important as a determinant of performance.

Certain product groups and certain whole sectors of manufacturing industry fail to achieve any significant coefficients whichever performance measure is applied. These are product groups 5, 8, 11, 23, 25, 27, 30, 31, 40, 41, 42, 46, 52/55, 57, 61, 63, 67, 68, 78, and the Chemical and Instrument Engineering sectors.

Those sectors of manufacturing industry which in general seem to benefit from the availability of services vary, as already suggested, with the dependent variable used. With QQQQQQ, the Clothing, Bricks Pottery and Glass, and Paper Printing and Publishing industries are all well represented by product groups with significant coefficients on PCOMPI. In other sectors PCOMPI records fewer significant coefficients.

With net output per head minus wages and salaries, no one sector except Printing and Publishing stands out as containing a large number of product groups with significant regression coefficients on PCOMPI in equation 3.

When performance is measured using the efficiency index, then besides the Clothing, Printing and Publishing and Bricks Pottery and Glass sectors which are significantly influenced by the availability of services, the Metal Manufacturing, Mechanical Engineering, Shipbuilding, and Timber and Furniture orders also show up very strongly. In particular of the nine product groups representing the Mechanical Engineering industry, no less than six recorded positive and significant regression coefficients for PCOMPI with EFFINN, five of which were significant at the 5% level or less: (product groups 29, 34, 37, 38, and 39). The Timber and Furniture sector also achieved significant coefficients at 1% in both product groups on PCOMPI.

It seems therefore that for a wide range of product groups, and sets of product groups, the availability of services associates strongly with improved manufacturing performance subregion to subregion.

(b) The labour pool

The size of the labour pool was measured by the log of the employees in the manufacturing industries in each subregion. The variable could also be taken as one general measure of the size of the subregion.

Table 9.2
Product groups recording significant regression coefficients on LNXXXI with QQQQQQ and QQQQWS and EFFINN as the dependent variables

Significant at	QQQQQQ	QQQQWS	EFFINN
1%	4, 80*	4, 80*	6, 28, 34, 64, 76, 79, 81, 84
5%	9, 11*, 48/49, 64, 70, 76, 81, 83	11*, 12*, 14*, 30*	4, 8, 9, 37, 39, 41, 48/49, 50, 71, 83, 86
10%	8, 12*, 14*, 26, 37, 74, 79	9, 38*, 48/49, 70, 76, 83	14, 38, 40, 52/55, 68*, 72

(* = negative coefficient)

Table 9.2 shows that those product groups for which LNXXXI seemed to have a significant influence on performance measured by QQQQWS tended to be influenced to a slightly greater extent when performance was measured by net output per head. There were however some product groups common to only one dependent variable which achieved significant results with LNXXXI. Whilst some pattern could be identified between the results with QQQQQQ and QQQQWS, EFFINN produced a quite different set of product groups having significant coefficients on LNXXXI.

Overall six product groups obtained significant regression coefficients with all three performance measures. These were product groups 4, 9, 14, 48/49, 76, and 83. In all cases (excepting product group 14) the coefficients had positive signs. In product group14 the sign changed from positive with EFFINN to negative with QQQQQQ and QQQQWS. This group of product groups does not represent any one manufacturing sector in particular although product groups 4 and 9 are both food manufacturing groups.

As Table 9.2 shows, the signs on the significant coefficients tend to be positive, although with QQQQWS measuring performance, in six of the twelve product groups with significant coefficients on LNXXXI, the sign is negative. This suggests potential diseconomies are significant for some industries at least using certain performance measures. Negative and significant coefficients were recorded for product groups 11, 12, 14 and 80 with both QQQQQQ and QQQQWS. Thus in the Drinks industry for example large labour pools characteristic of large urban areas seem to be significantly and negatively related to industrial performance. Overall, those product groups which record negative coefficients (11, 12, 14, 30, 38, 68 and 80) are by and large groups concerned with the manufacture of heavy bulky products: Food, Drink, Machine Tools, Non Electrical Machinery, Leather and Fur, and Timber and Wood products. It is possible that in large agglomerations congestion imposes a significant cost on the performance of these industries. These product groups also tend to have small average numbers employed per establishment or a wide spread of plant sizes, and it could therefore be reasonably argued that for these product groups large labour pools are unlikely to be important.

Those product groups which seem to benefit by the presence of either the advantages associated with operating with a large urban area, or by being in close proximity to a large and available labour supply tend to be in the Food, Bricks Pottery and Glass, and Paper Printing and Publishing sectors, when QQQQQQ is used to measure performance. Only the coefficient in product group 4 is however significant at 1%. With QQQQWS only individual product groups identify themselves rather than sectors. With EFFINN a much wider range of manufacturing orders appears to be significantly influenced in their performance by LNXXXI. In particular, Food, Mechanical Engineering, Instrument Engineering, Vehicles, Bricks Pottery Glass, Paper Printing and Publishing, and other manufacturing industries all have at least half of their products recording positive and significant regression coefficients on LNXXXI.

An appraisal of the product groups making up these particular sectors does not provide any strong causality hypotheses. For example, since LNXXXI is a potential measure of labour availability it would have been reasonable to assume that those product groups employing high numbers of workers per establishment would be likely to benefit most from the availability of a large labour pool. This does not appear to be a valid explanation of the groups picked. This could possibly suggest that LNXXXI is acting more as a general proxy for the size of agglomeration than as a good measure of labour availability.

Those product groups which failed to achieve significant coefficients on LNXXXI are far greater in number in the case of QQQQWS measuring performance than with EFFINN. With QQQQWS seven sectors of manufacturing failed to record significant coefficients: Chemicals, Metal Manufacture, Instrument Engineering, Electrical Engineering, Vehicles, Other Metals and Textiles. In addition numerous other individual product groups within sectors achieved no significant coefficients. With QQQQQQ, four sectors namely Chemicals, Electrical Engineering, Other Metal Goods and Vehicles, failed in all their product groups to record significant coefficients. With EFFINN, three sectors failed: Chemicals, Electrical Engineering, and Other Metal Goods.

It seems therefore, that the agglomeration measure used reflects a factor capable of acting as an advantage for certain groups in the manufacturing industry and as a potential diseconomy for others. In addition it seems that any conclusions on the significance of LNXXXI for the performance of any industry should distinguish clearly how that performance is measured. Finally it appears that LNXXXI could well be acting less like a measure of labour availability and more like a general agglomeration proxy variable since LNXXXI seems to be no more important for product groups with a large number of employees per establishment than for those with smaller average plant sizes.

(c) Relative labour availability

The labour availability in relation to the overall population size of the subregion was measured by the number of manufacturing employees as a proportion of population size in each subregion.

Table 9.3
Product groups recording significant regression coefficients on XXIPOP with QQQQQQ, QQQQWS and EFFINN as the dependent variables

Significant at	QQQQQQ	QQQQWS	EFFINN
1%	9, 48/49, 76		
5%	26, 46*, 79, 80*, 82*	9, 46*, 48/49, 76, 79, 80*, 82*	14, 28, 41, 48/49, 64, 76, 78
10%	6*, 11*, 47*, 74*, 78	11*, 47*, 70, 78	9, 35, 47*, 74*, 86

(* = negative coefficient)

XXIPOP was introduced to measure the relative size of the labour pool in each subregion. As Table 9.3 shows this factor is only significantly related to manufacturing performance at 1% in three different product groups 9, 48/49, and 76, and then only when performance is measured by net output per head. The sign in each case is positive. There are, in addition, far fewer significant coefficients recorded with XXIPOP than LNXXXI, and also a much higher incidence of negative coefficients, suggesting possible diseconomies of scale for those groups concerned. It seems therefore that XXIPOP has measured something rather different than that measured by LNXXXI, and hopefully XXIPOP has focussed more closely upon labour availability than it has upon more general size proxies. There is nevertheless an overlap still existing between these two independent variables (LNXXXI and XXIPOP) shown by product groups achieving significant coefficients with the like signs for both these independent variables.

The results from XXIPOP being applied in equation 6 show that product groups 9, 48/49, 76, and 78 recorded positive and significant coefficients with each manufacturing performance measure. Various other product groups also recorded positive significant coefficients on XXIPOP, mostly with EFFINN as the dependent variable. These product groups are distributed across all sectors of manufacturing industry except Chemicals, Vehicles, Other Metal Goods and Newspapers, Publishing, and Paper Manufacture.

Product groups 6, 11, 46, 47, 74, 80 and 82 each recorded significant and negative coefficients, generally with QQQQQQ, and QQQQWS as dependent variables. These product groups represent many different manufacturing sectors: Food, Electrical Engineering, Bricks, Timber, and Paper Manufacturing. Product groups 11 and 80 also recorded negative and significant coefficients on LNXXXI. These product groups therefore achieve higher net output per head figures in areas which are not strong in manufacturing, and for product groups 11 and 80 in smaller subregions.

The XXIPOP variable seems to have been more selective in its effect than LNXXXI, and as such recorded fewer significant coefficients in total, yet more negative significant coefficients as well. In addition the level of significance of the coefficients was lower than when LNXXXI was tested. It seems possible from the results of these two variables that XXIPOP has tended to measure relative labour availability for manufacturing more successfully than LNXXXI, and as a consequence returned few significant results. This could reflect the diminishing importance of strictly manpower considerations for manufacturing industry at a time when the mechanisation of standardised production processes was well under way. In addition the relative high number of negative coefficients could be suggesting that the congested conditions in the relatively large labour market areas are more than outweighing the benefits of labour availability for certain product groups, or that these groups require a labour force that is more service/professionally orientated and less manufacturing orientated.

(d) The skills of the labour force

The availability of labour skills was measured by the numbers of skilled manual workers in each subregion. Table 9.4 shows at a glance that as a measure of performance EFFINN enables SKILMN to achieve many more significant coefficients than either QQQQWS or QQQQQQ.

Table 9.4
Product groups recording significant regression coefficients on SKILMN with QQQQQQ, QQQQWS, and EFFINN as the dependent performance variable

Significant at	QQQQQQ	QQQQWS	EFFINN
1%	4, 37, 64, 74, 83, 70	4	6, 34, 50, 64, 70, 71, 74, 76, 79, 80, 81, 83
5%	8, 26, 59, 73, 76, 81	8, 37, 59, 64, 73, 74, 81, 83	8, 12, 26, 28, 38, 37, 39, 59, 69, 72, 73
10%	9, 50, 72*, 79	12*, 14*, 30*, 45, 70, 80	9, 14, 29, 35, 47, 48/49, 82, 84, 85, 86

(* = negative coefficient)

Overall, with each of the performance measures the number of skilled manual workers tends to record positive rather than negative significant regression coefficients. The least significant coefficients, and the smallest number of positive and largest number of negative coefficients for SKILMN occur when QQQQWS is used to measure performance. Negative coefficients in product groups 12, 14, 30, 80 correspond to the negative coefficients when LNXXXI was being tested as an independent variable. In these product groups at least therefore, if LNXXXI is unsuccessful in measuring labour availability, then it seems as if SKILMN could also be acting as a size proxy variable, rather than character of workforce or size of labour pool availability measure. The product groups with positive coefficients on SKILMN do not coincide to the same degree with those on LNXXXI when QQQQWS is the dependent variable. Product groups here with SKILMN coefficients which are positive and significant occur in a variety of sectors, notably Food, and Printing and Publishing. Far more significant coefficients occur when QQQQQQ is the dependent variable. The product groups which record these positive significant regression coefficients for SKILMN coincide very closely with the product groups having positive and significant coefficients on LNXXXI. Again therefore it seems that SKILMN could be measuring only labour availability in general or be just a size measure in disguise.

By far the greatest number of significant coefficients are recorded on SKILMN when EFFINN is the dependent variable. Overall thirty-three of the fifty-three product groups achieve positive and significant coefficients, of which no less than twelve are significant at 1%, and another eleven at 5%. These thirty-three product groups, for which performance is positively related to the size of the skilled manual labour force in the subregion, represent every manufacturing sector except Chemicals, and Instrument Engineering. Those sectors which are particularly well represented (at least two thirds of the product groups in that sector have a significant coefficient on SKILMN at the 10% level) are Drink, Metal Manufacture, Mechanical Engineering, Shipbuilding, Clothing, Bricks Pottery Glass, Timber, Paper Printing and Publishing, and other manufacturing industries. Are these sectors where skills are at a premium, and a resident labour force with traditional skills is likely to benefit the performance of these sectors? It is not possible at this stage to pursue this question but it is certainly an area for future work. It is to be noted however that of the thirty-three product groups which achieved significant coefficients on SKILMN with EFFINN, no less than twenty are product groups which achieved significant coefficients on LNXXXI, out of a total of twenty-five. It seems yet again therefore that SKILMN may well be measuring either overall labour availability or agglomeration size, as well as character and availability of the labour force. There are however thirteen different product groups which achieved significant coefficients on SKILMN and not on LNXXXI with EFFINN as the dependent variable and these are product groups 12, 26, 29, 35, 47, 59, 69, 70, 73, 74, 80, 82, and 85. These represent a wide variety of manufacturing sectors, but nevertheless are numerous enough with coefficients mostly significant at 5% or less to suggest that with EFFINN as the performance measure, SKILMN is acting as a viable agglomeration proxy variable measuring more than simply agglomeration size.

Overall therefore it seems that the number of skilled workers can be regarded as a useful agglomeration proxy variable and produces many more positive and significant coefficients than XXIPOP or LNXXXI. This suggests that the availability of skills are very much more important than the availability of manpower <u>per se</u>, to manufacturing industry.

(e) The relative pool of skilled workers

The relative availability of skilled manual labour was measured by the proportion of skilled manual workers to total manufacturing employees in each subregion.

Table 9.5
Product groups recording significant regression coefficients on SKLXXI with QQQQQQ, QQQQWS and EFFINN as the dependent performance variable

Significant at	QQQQQQ	QQQQWS	EFFINN
1%	48/49*, 76*	48/49*, 80	28*,76*, 78*, 79*
5%	9*, 46, 79*, 80	9*, 46, 76*	39*, 40*, 48/49*, 57*, 86*
10%	4*, 78*	4*, 70, 79*, 82, 83*, 85*	35, 52*, 68, 72*

(* = negative coefficient)

Table 9.5 shows that with QQQQQQ as the dependent variable only two product groups, 80 and 46, recorded positive and significant coefficients on SKLXXI. These groups also had negative coefficients on XXIPOP suggesting the possible advantages for these groups of operating within a relatively small manufacturing labour market, or conversely a large non manufacturing labour market. With QQQQWS, product group 70 also recorded a positive and significant coefficient. In these product groups therefore; Electrical Goods, Women's Outerwear, and Timber Manufacturing, an available and highly skilled workforce seems to be beneficial to performance of the industry in general. This pattern is however the exception. In product groups 48/49, 76 and 79 with QQQQQQ, QQQQWS and EFFINN, negative and significant coefficients generally at the 1% level were recorded on SKLXXI. For these groups therefore it seems that large pools of unskilled labour in the workforce are very necessary. The regression coefficients on LNXXXI and XXIPOP also suggested that these product groups required large pools of manufacturing labour to improve manufacturing performance. Negative and significant coefficients were also recorded for two product groups in the Food sector with QQQQQQ and QQQQWS: namely product groups 4 and 9. These are two product groups where unskilled labour might well be expected to be required in the Mechanised Food Processing and Packaging industries.

With the efficiency index used to measure manufacturing performance product group 28 Copper and Brass, and product group 78 Other Building Materials are two further product groups which are identified as having negative and significant regression coefficients at 1% on SKLXXI. Again therefore a highly skilled workforce acts as a positive external diseconomy for these manufacturing groups, possibly reflecting the shortage of available unskilled labour. Negative coefficients on SKLXXI with EFFINN are also recorded in a selection of other manufacturing sectors including the Aircraft industry with its very high number of employees per plant, the Mechanical and Instrument Engineering industries, and the Clothing industry.

In general SKLXXI does not achieve a very large number of significant coefficients. In those product groups where performance is significantly related to the proportion of the labour force which is classified as skilled however, it does appear that the relative availability of unskilled workers is far more commonly beneficial to performance than the relative availability of skilled workers, given a particular labour pool.

If these results are compared with those for SKILMN it can be seen that those product groups which achieve significant negative coefficients on SKLXXI and positive significant regression coefficients on SKILMN with the three different performance variables are as follows:-

with QQQQQQ product groups 4, 9, 76, 79
with QQQQWS product groups 4, 83
with EFFINN product groups 28, 39, 48/49, 72, 76, 79, 86

It might appear that these two results are contradictory. In fact it means that in these product groups manufacturing performance improves the larger the number of skilled manual workers in the sub-region in total, but also the larger the proportion of unskilled manual workers in the workforce. For this to be true the overall workforce size has also to be positively related to performance. This occurs in each of the product groups with the appropriate dependent variable. Thus while these different proxy variables for agglomeration economies may appear to both overlap and conflict, it does seem that they are capable of both measuring different effects and that these effects are capable of explanation.

(f) Rural versus urban

Table 9.6
Product groups recording significant regression coefficients on URBRUR with QQQQQQ, QQQQWS and EFFINN as the dependent performance variable

Significant at	QQQQQQ	QQQQWS	EFFINN
1%	48/49*, 80	80	
5%	4*, 11, 14, 30, 38, 52/55	4*, 9*, 14, 25, 30, 38, 48/49*, 52/55*	69, 76*
10%	9*, 35, 37*, 69, 76*	11, 37*, 70*, 73	4*, 23*, 35, 61* 68, 70, 83, 84*

(* = negative coefficient)

Negative coefficients imply that performance, however it is measured, is greater in urban areas. It seems therefore from Table 9.6 that few product groups are significantly influenced in their performance by operating within urban locations per se. Only product group 4 (Grain Milling) recorded significant negative coefficients on URBRUR with all three performance variables. Product groups 9, 37, and 48/49 recorded negative and significant coefficients with both net output per head and net output per head minus wages and salaries. Product group 76 (Glass) is also positively influenced in its performance by urban operating environments when EFFINN and QQQQQQ are used to measure performance. Other product groups for which urban locations seem to be beneficial are Aircraft Manufacture, Chemicals, Women's Tailored Outerwear, Yarns and Thread, and Rubber Manufactures. In most cases those product groups which recorded negative and significant coefficients on URBRUR also recorded positive and significant coefficients on many of the proxy agglomeration economy variables. This is to be expected since agglomeration economies are likely to accrue, by and large, in the more urban subregions. There were however numerous product groups in which significant and positive regression coefficients were recorded for the agglomeration economy variables and for which the URBRUR effect was insignificant (e.g. product groups 64, 74, 81 and 83 with QQQQQQ, product group 83 with QQQQWS, and numerous product groups with EFFINN).

Those product groups which recorded positive coefficients on URBRUR, and for which rural locations appear to benefit performance were similar when QQQQQQ and QQQQWS were used as performance measures. For example, product group 80 (Timber and Wood Manufactures) as one might expect, recorded positive and significant coefficients on URBRUR at the 1% level with both dependent variables. Other product groups for which rural locations appear to favour performance are Other Food Products (product group 11), Soft Drinks and Cider (product group 14), Machine Tools (product group 30), and Non Electrical Machinery (product group 38). Some of these results appear to be more plausible than others. It might be that the results have been biased by new plants with modern machinery setting up in out of town locations and making it appear that certain industries perform better in rural locations when in fact their performance only reflects the modernity of their production processes. There is unfortunately no way of avoiding this inbuilt bias without a clear picture of investment in new plant and machinery. This we do not possess.

(g) Declining regions

The percentage unemployment rate, averaged for the years 1966-1970, has been interpreted as reflecting on older capital stock and social infrastructure. It corresponds closely with the definition of the Assisted Areas in 1968 as seen in the map in chapter six.

Table 9.7 overleaf shows clearly that negative regression coefficients on XXXXX9 occur more or less consistently with each dependent performance variable. The number of product groups achieving significant coefficients is large and this suggests that for many different manufacturing industries the industrial environment in which they operate is important and that the older industrial locations with outdated capital and high unemployment are not conducive to improved manufacturing performance. This is in spite of the new capital investment attracted to these areas by regional economic development policies. Those product groups which record negative and significant coefficients with all three performance measures are product groups 4, 26, 31, 37, 48/49, 52-55, 68, and 79.

Table 9.7
Product groups recording significant regression coefficients on XXXXX9 with QQQQQQ, QQQQWS and EFFINN as the dependent performance variable

Significant at	QQQQQQ	QQQQWS	EFFINN
1%	31*, 48/49*, 52/55*, 68*, 79*	31*, 39*, 68*, 79*, 80	11*, 37*, 48/49*, 52-55*, 78*
5%	4*, 5*, 26*, 37*, 39*, 76*, 80, 85*	4*, 48/49*, 52-55*, 85*	5*, 9*, 40*, 64*, 68*, 71*, 72, 79*, 81, 86*
10%	35*, 71*, 78*, 83*	11, 25*, 26*, 35*, 37*, 76*, 83*	4*, 25*, 26*, 31*, 50*, 63*, 67*, 73*, 74*

(* = negative coefficient)

Individual manufacturing sectors which appear to be influenced in a number of their product groups by the age of capital variable are the Mechanical Engineering industry and the Shipbuilding industry with QQQQQQ and QQQQWS measuring performance, and the Food, Vehicle, Textile, Clothing, and Bricks Pottery and Glass industries when performance is measured using the efficiency index. These sectors include many of the older established manufacturing industries of the United Kingdom, which will of course be located predominantly in the older, more depressed industrial conurbations.

Although the significance attached to the XXXXX9 coefficient varies with the performance measure, Shipbuilding, Vehicles, Industrial Plant, Pumps and Valves, and Furniture and Bedding all recorded significant coefficients on XXXXX9 at the 1% level with two of the three dependent variables. Only the Drink, Electrical Engineering and Other Metal Goods sectors failed to record any significant coefficients on XXXXX9. In these sectors therefore the quality of the industrial environment is not a significant factor.

These results suggest quite conclusively that the unemployment rate cannot be used as a potential labour availability variable, but is quite consistently significant in explaining a negative relationship with performance in terms of the environment of the traditional industrial centres of the country.

2 COMBINING THE AGGLOMERATION VARIABLES: EQUATIONS 8, 9 and 10

Tables 9.8 to 9.16 summarise the regression results from three different equations, each estimated using different dependent variables for fifty-three different manufacturing product groups. There is a considerable amount of information contained within these tables, although this section aims to summarise only the major patterns which emerge from the regression analysis, in order to identify the broad conclusions which follow from the tables.

Tables 9.8 to 9.16 present the number of each product group achieving significant coefficients at the 1%, 5% and 10% level, on the independent variables in each equation (8, 9 or 10), and with each dependent variable (QQQQQQ, QQQQWS, EFFINN). In this way the results can be compared, one group with another, through the success of one independent variable with another in different equations, or in the same equation using different dependent variables.

The results are summarised, first with respect to the constant term and size of plant variable (LNNNQQ), and then individually by the four proxy variables for agglomeration economies.

(a) Constant terms and size of plant variables

As Tables 9.8 to 9.16 show, taking each dependent variable at a time, the constant terms and size of plant variables in equations 8, 9 and 10 tend to record significant coefficients for similar product groups. With EFFINN (Tables 9.10, 9.13, 9.16) all the product groups record constant terms which are positive and significant at 1% in all equations. With QQQQQQ (Tables 9.8, 9.11, 9.14) similar product groups record significant coefficients at 10% or more in equations 8, 9 and 10, however different product groups are represented at the different significance levels (i.e. at 1%, 5% and 10%). The product groups which are represented at 10% or more amount to over half the manufacturing product groups in total in each equation, and represent all sectors of manufacturing production. With QQQQWS (Tables 9.9, 9.12, 9.15) less than half the product groups achieve significant constant terms at 10%, very few product groups achieve constants which are significant at 1%, and of those product groups which are successful, they vary between one equation and the next.

The size of plant variable records significant and generally positive coefficients with EFFINN as the dependent variable, in virtually the same product groups in each of the equations (8, 9 and 10). These product groups represent about 80% of the manufacturing groups analysed.

With QQQQQQ as the dependent variable a very similar set of product groups records significant and positive coefficients at 10% or more on the size of plant variable in equations 8, 9 and 10. These also represent 80% of manufacturing industry analysed. The Electrical Engineering industry and Other Metal Goods industry are both unrepresented.

Table 9.8
Product groups recording significant coefficients in equation 8 with QQQQQQ

Significance levels	10%	5%	1%
Constant	23, 30, 40, 74, 82	12, 42, 46, 47, 52/55, 57, 64*, 67, 71, 79, 84, 86	5, 26, 31, 37, 39, 45, 48/9, 50, 59, 61, 72, 78, 80, 83
Size of plant	23, 39, 70	8, 12, 30, 40, 41, 50, 71, 76, 78, 86	5, 6, 9, 11, 14, 25, 26, 28, 34, 35, 37, 38, 45*, 63, 64, 67, 68, 69, 73, 74, 79, 80, 82, 83, 85
LNXXXI	8, 12*, 23*, 37*, 67*, 73, 80*, 82*	46*, 64, 83	61
PCOMPI	50, 70, 71, 81	46, 63, 67, 72, 74, 82	37, 61*, 80, 83
XXXXX9	4*, 30*, 37*, 46*, 71*, 73*, 76*, 85*	5*, 26*, 39*, 48/49*, 52/55*, 78*	25*, 31*, 61, 68*, 79*
URBRUR	29, 30, 52/55, 68, 69	14, 23*, 25, 38, 61	64, 73, 83

(* = negative coefficient)

Table 9.9
Product groups recording significant coefficients in equation 8 with QQQQWS

Significance levels	10%	5%	1%
Constant	12, 23, 47, 50, 52/55, 67, 78, 84	11*, 31, 45, 46, 59, 64*, 69, 71, 73*, 74, 80, 83	48/49, 61*
Size of plant	8, 23, 30, 40, 76, 78, 83, 86	6, 9, 26, 41, 63, 67, 70, 79	4, 5, 11, 12, 14, 25, 28, 34, 35, 37, 38, 39, 64, 68, 73, 80, 82, 85
LNXXXI	12*, 23*, 37*, 67*	46*, 64, 73, 80*	61
PCOMPI	30*, 67, 84	46, 83	37, 61*
XXXXX9	4*, 5*, 30*, 35*, 63*, 76*	31*, 52/55*, 61, 85*	25*, 39*, 68*, 79*
URBRUR	68	23*, 25, 37*, 52/55	61, 64, 73

(* = negative coefficient)

Table 9.10
Product groups recording significant coefficients in equation 8 with EFFINN

Significance levels	10%	5%	1%
Constant	27	8	4, 5, 6, 9, 11, 12, 14, 23, 25, 26, 28, 29, 30, 31, 34, 35, 37, 38, 39, 40, 41, 42, 45, 46, 47, 48/49, 50, 52/55, 57, 59, 61, 63, 64, 67, 68, 69, 70, 71, 72, 73, 74, 75, 78, 79, 80, 81, 82, 83, 84, 85, 86
Size of plant	11, 31, 40, 41*, 63, 81, 84	26, 27, 28, 29, 30, 38, 46, 48/49, 50, 52/55, 61*, 85	4, 6, 8, 9, 14, 23, 25, 34, 37, 45*, 59, 64, 67, 68, 71, 73, 74, 78, 79, 80, 82, 83, 86
LNXXXI	14, 38, 39, 63*, 69, 71, 80, 85	8, 9, 28, 34, 61, 64, 68*, 70, 81, 83, 84	6
PCOMPI	63, 64, 72	12, 50, 68, 70, 71, 73, 74, 80, 82, 83	26, 61*
XXXXX9	4*, 26*, 31*, 40*, 64*, 67*, 73*, 86*	5*, 6*, 9*, 37*, 48/49*, 61, 68*, 72*, 79*, 81*	11*, 52/55*, 71*, 78*
URBRUR	14, 48/49, 63*, 81	6, 8, 11, 35, 38, 64, 78, 80	69, 70, 71, 83

(* = negative coefficient)

Table 9.11
Product groups recording significant coefficients in equation 9 with QQQQQQ

Significance levels	10%	5%	1%
Constant	12, 23, 27, 29, 67, 73	4, 30, 37, 40, 42, 68, 76, 78, 79, 82, 84	5, 26, 31, 39, 45, 46, 47, 48/49, 50, 52/55, 57, 59, 69, 71, 72, 74, 80, 83, 86
Size of plant	39, 76, 84	8, 12, 23, 29, 30, 40, 41, 50, 63, 70, 71, 78, 86	4, 5, 6, 9, 11, 14, 25, 26, 28, 34, 35, 37, 38, 45*, 64, 67, 68, 73, 74, 79, 80, 82, 83, 85
XXIPOP	52/55, 67*, 84*	9, 39*, 46*, 47*, 70, 71*, 76, 78, 79	82*
PCOMPI	4, 26, 35, 63	23*, 50, 59, 69, 72, 73, 81	37, 64, 70, 74, 83
XXXXX9	26*, 30*, 37*, 73*, 80*, 83*, 85*	4*, 5*, 31*, 39*, 48/49*, 52/55*, 71*, 82*	25*, 68*, 79*
URBRUR	4*, 5, 25, 38, 70	23*, 30, 52/55, 64, 73, 78, 80, 83	14

(* = negative coefficient)

Table 9.12
Product groups recording significant coefficients in equation 9 with QQQQWS

Significance levels	10%	5%	1%
Constant	9*, 52/55, 63	11*, 31, 38*, 46, 47, 48/49, 50, 69, 83, 86	39, 45, 59, 71
Size of plant	8, 23, 29, 39, 40, 84, 86	6, 9, 12, 26, 41, 67, 70, 74, 83	4, 5, 11, 14, 25, 28, 34, 35, 37, 38, 63, 64, 68, 73, 79, 80, 82, 85
XXIPOP	47*, 74*, 76, 78, 84*	9, 23*, 39*, 46*, 71*, 79, 82*	
PCOMPI	45, 73	63, 64, 74, 81	4, 37, 83
XXXXX9	4*, 5*, 9, 30*, 48/49*, 63, 80, 82*	31*, 52/55*, 79*, 85*	25*, 39*, 68*
URBRUR	4*, 5, 14, 38, 42, 59*, 78, 80	23*, 25, 30, 52/55, 64, 73, 79	

(* = negative coefficient)

Table 9.13
Product groups recording significant coefficients in equation 9 with EFFINN

Significance levels	10%	5%	1%
Constant			4, 5, 6, 8, 9, 11, 12, 14, 23, 25, 26, 27, 28, 29, 30, 31, 34, 35, 37, 38, 39, 40, 41, 42, 45, 46, 47, 48/49, 50, 52/55, 57, 59, 61, 63, 64, 67, 68, 69, 70, 71, 73, 74, 76, 78, 79, 80, 81, 82, 83, 84, 85, 86
Size of plant	11, 27, 31, 40, 41*, 61*	28, 30, 46, 74, 85	4, 6, 8, 9, 14, 23, 25, 26, 29, 34, 38, 37, 45*, 48/49, 50, 52/55, 59, 64, 67, 68, 71, 72, 73, 78, 79, 80, 82, 83, 86
XXIPOP	23*, 34, 47*, 48/49, 67*, 78	14, 28, 42*, 64, 70, 73*, 80	82*
PCOMPI	14, 25, 39, 48/49, 59, 82, 84	12, 28, 29, 35, 38, 72, 73, 79, 81	6, 26, 34, 50, 64, 69, 70, 71, 74, 80, 83
XXXXX9	4*, 9*, 23*, 31*, 40*, 86*	5*, 11*, 37*, 48/49*, 67*, 68*, 72*, 73*, 79*, 81*	52/55*, 71*, 78
URBRUR	4*, 8, 61*, 64, 71, 81, 82	11, 14, 23, 42*, 48/49, 69, 80, 83	70,78

(* = negative coefficient)

Table 9.14
Product groups recording significant coefficients
in equation 10 with QQQQQQ

Significance levels	10%	5%	1%
Constant	29, 41, 46, 68, 70, 85	4, 30, 37, 40, 47, 52/55, 86	5, 26, 31, 39, 42, 45, 48/49, 50, 57, 59, 69, 71, 72, 74, 76, 78, 79, 80, 83
Size of plant	29, 39, 52/55, 59, 78, 86	8, 12, 23, 30, 40, 41, 50, 70, 71, 76, 84	4, 5, 6, 9, 11 14, 25, 26, 28, 34, 35, 37, 38, 45*, 63, 64, 67, 68, 73, 74, 79, 80, 82, 83, 85
SKLXXI	9*, 73, 74, 78*, 82, 83*	23*, 59, 71, 76*, 79*, 84	46
PCOMPI	4, 35, 46, 52/55, 82	50, 59, 63, 69, 70, 72, 73, 81	37, 64, 78, 83
XXXXX9	4*, 30*, 37*, 80, 82*	5*, 25*, 26*, 31*, 39*, 48/49*, 52/55*, 71*, 73*	46*, 68*, 79*
URBRUR	5, 25, 30, 69, 73, 78, 79, 84*	11, 14, 23*, 38, 52/55, 80, 83	46*

(* = negative coefficient)

Table 9.15
Product groups recording significant coefficients
in equation 10 with QQQQWS

Significance levels	10%	5%	1%
Constant	14*, 23, 26, 28*, 34, 63*, 69, 72	11*, 31, 45, 50, 59, 76, 78, 79	39, 48/49, 83
Size of plant	8, 23, 39, 67, 76, 86	6, 9, 12, 26, 40, 41, 70, 74, 79, 83, 84	4, 5, 11, 14, 25, 28, 34, 35, 37, 38, 63, 64, 68, 73, 80, 82, 85
XXIPOP	9*, 40, 74, 76*, 79*, 82, 83	23, 39, 71, 84	46
PCOMPI	73	4, 45, 63, 64, 74, 81	37, 83
XXXXX9	4*, 5*, 11, 30*, 52/55*, 63, 71*, 73*, 80, 82*, 84*, 85*	25*, 26*, 31*, 68*, 79*	39*, 46*
URBRUR	5, 11, 14, 25*, 40*, 71*, 79, 84*	23*, 30, 38, 46*, 52/55, 73	

(* = negative coefficient)

Table 9.16
Product groups recording significant coefficients in equation 10 with EFFINN

Significance levels	10%	5%	1%
Constant			4, 5, 6, 8, 9, 11, 12, 14, 23, 25, 26, 27, 28, 29, 30, 31, 34, 35, 38, 37, 39, 40, 41, 42, 45, 46, 47, 48/49, 50, 52/55, 57, 59, 61, 63, 64, 67, 68, 69, 70, 71, 72, 73, 74, 76, 78, 79, 80, 81, 82, 83, 84, 85, 86
Size of plant	27, 31, 40, 41*, 76, 84	30, 46, 74, 85	4, 6, 8, 9, 14, 23, 25, 26, 28, 29, 34, 38, 37, 45*, 48/49, 50, 52/55, 59, 64, 67, 68, 71, 73, 78, 79, 80, 82, 83, 86
SKILXI	40*, 69*, 70, 74	14*, 39*, 59, 68, 76*, 79*	28*, 57*, 73, 78*
PCOMPI	28, 29, 39, 47, 82	12, 35, 38, 59, 69, 72, 76, 79, 81	6, 26, 34, 50, 64, 70, 71, 73, 74, 80, 83
XXXXX9	4*, 9*, 28, 63*, 67*, 72*	5*, 11*, 37*, 48/49*, 81*	52/55*, 68*, 71*, 73*, 78*
URBRUR	8, 14, 71, 81	11, 28, 48/49, 57, 61*, 80	69, 70, 78

(* = negative coefficient)

With QQQQWS as the dependent variable about 60% of the product groups record positive and significant coefficients on the size of plant variable. As with QQQQQQ and EFFINN, the same product groups tend to be represented in each equation recording the same level of significance on LNNNQQ. These product groups represent many sectors of manufacturing industry. However there is a noticeable gap in the range between product groups 41 and 63, for which no significant size of plant coefficients were recorded in equations 8, 9 or 10 with QQQQWS as the dependent variable.

(b) Agglomeration variables

Tables 9.8 to 9.16 show that the number of product groups recording significant coefficients on the agglomeration economy proxy variables in these equations is far fewer than on either the size of plant or constant terms.

Of all the agglomeration proxy variables, the greatest number of significant coefficients are recorded on XXXXX9, and the vast majority of these have a negative sign. Overall there is no clear picture as to which product groups achieve significant coefficients at least at the 10% level with the different dependent variables in the three different equations. Five product groups achieve significant coefficients consistently. These are product groups 4, 5, 52/55, 68 and 79. Others, namely product groups 25, 30, 31, 39 and 85 achieve significant coefficients in all equations with QQQQWS and QQQQQQ. Another set of product groups, 48/49, 71 and 73, achieve significant coefficients in all equations with QQQQQQ and EFFINN as the performance measure. There are other product groups which only achieve significant coefficients consistently with one dependent variable, e.g. product group 63 with QQQQWS, product groups 26 and 37 with QQQQQQ, and product groups 9, 11, 67, 78, and 81 with EFFINN.

Product groups with significant coefficients on XXXXX9 which are significant at the 1% level tend to be represented on more than one occasion,out of the nine possible. For example, while eleven different product groups record at least one significant regression coefficient on XXXXX9 at the 1% level, product group 25 records a significant coefficient on XXXXX9 at 1% on four occasions, product group 39, on three occasions, product groups 52/55 on three occasions, product group 68 on no less than six occasions, product groups 71 and 78 on three, and product group 79 on four occasions. No one equation and no one dependent variable seems to be more successful than the others in terms of the number of significant coefficients recorded on XXXXX9. The product groups with significant coefficients on XXXXX9 in equations 8, 9, and 10, represent all sectors of manufacturing industry and no clear sectoral breakdown seems appropriate.

PCOMPI recorded the second highest number of significant regression coefficients, over the fifty-three different product groups. By far the greatest number of these significant results occurred when the efficiency index was adopted as the dependent variable and of these, a higher proportion of coefficients was significant at the 1% level than occurred when using QQQQQQ or QQQQWS as dependent variables. The least number of significant coefficients was recorded with QQQQWS. In virtually all cases the significant coefficients had positive signs, suggesting that the existence of service industries close at hand benefits the performance of all those product groups concerned.

Most of the manufacturing product groups achieve at least one significant coefficient in PCOMPI in the nine potential equations available. Those product groups which are never represented however are product groups 5, 8, 9, 11, 27, 31, 40, 41, 42, 57, 85, and 86. Of these, the first four represent the Food industry and 40 and 41 represent the Instrument Engineering industry; the others are from a selection of manufacturing sectors. Certain product groups achieve a high number of significant coefficients at the 1% level, notably product groups 83, 37 and 64, recording seven, six and four significant regression coefficients on PCOMPI at 1%, respectively. Others are product groups 26, 61, 70, 74 and 80, each recording three significant coefficients at 1%. It seems therefore that in these product groups especially the proximity to and the availability of service industries are particularly beneficial to performance. With EFFINN as the dependent variable, the Clothing industry product groups in particular record a high incidence of significant coefficients at the 1% level.

The third and most successful agglomeration economy proxy variable in equations 8, 9 and 10 is URBRUR, measured in terms of the number of significant regression coefficients which it records throughout the fifty-three different product groups. In most cases the significant coefficients have positive signs suggesting that performance is improved outside of urban locations for the product groups concerned. The product groups themselves however present no clear picture, varying as they do both with the equation being estimated, and the dependent variable. Some of the product groups record significant coefficients on URBRUR in equations with different dependent variables but the same independent variables, others do the exact reverse. A mixture of different processes seems to be at work and these seem near impossible to disentangle.

Overall the greatest consistency is in the product groups recording significant coefficients on URBRUR with EFFINN. In this case the actual equations seem to matter less than the dependent variable. Product groups 8, 11, 14, 48, 69, 70, 71, 78, 80 and 81 all record positive and significant coefficients in all equations on URBRUR.

With QQQQWS and QQQQQQ as the dependent variables however the independent variables accompanying URBRUR seem to be more of a determinant of which product groups record a significant URBRUR coefficient than the dependent variables themselves. Product groups 14, 23, 25, 30, 38, 52/55, and 73 do however record significant coefficients in at least five of the six different potential equations using QQQQQQ and QQQQWS as dependent variables. A wide range of product groups (9, 12, 26, 27, 31, 34, 39, 41, 45, 47, 50, 67, 72, 74, 76, 85, 86) from most manufacturing sectors except Chemicals, Shipbuilding, Other Metal Goods, Timber and Furniture, and Paper Printing and Publishing record no significant coefficients on URBRUR in equations 8, 9 or 10, with any of the three dependent performance variables. Equally however all sectors are represented by at least one product group with significant coefficients on URBRUR.

Significant coefficients at 1% on URBRUR are not very common. They are recorded in a mixture of different product groups, mostly however concentrated in the Clothing and Textile industries. Product groups 64, 69, 70, 71, and 73 record a total of eleven significant coefficients on URBRUR at the 1% level out of an overall total of seventeen. These are all positive in their sign.

LNXXXI, XXIPOP, and SKLXXI were each used in this study as slightly different measures of labour availability as previously explained. The former is also very likely to act as a proxy for the size of the agglomerations within the subregions, whilst XXIPOP and SKLXXI are relative measures of availability of labour in general and skilled labour in particular. The first was used in equation 8, the second in equation 9, and the third in equation 10, each along with PCOMPI, XXXXX9 and URBRUR, as the independent variables upon which QQQQWS, QQQQQQ and EFFINN were regressed.

Exactly as one would expect, there is little similarity between the list of product groups achieving significant coefficients on LNXXXI, XXIPOP and SKLXXI with the different dependent variables, that is not to say however that there is no overlap. Whilst, also as might be expected, there is some similarity in the list of product groups achieving significant coefficients in equations using the same set of independent, but different dependent variables.

Looking at the results equation by equation, it seems that in equation 8 only product groups 61 and 64, both in the Textile sector, record consistent positive significant coefficients on LNXXXI, with all three dependent variables. There are however a number of product groups which achieve significant coefficients with both QQQQQQ and QQQQWS, on LNXXXI, in equation 8. These are product groups 12, 23, 37, 46, 67 and 80, all of which also record negative coefficients suggesting certain diseconomies of agglomeration or the requirement of these product groups for non manufacturing labour, in close proximity. Product group 73 records positive and significant coefficients with both performance variables. With EFFINN the signs on the coefficients are mainly positive (in striking contrast with QQQQWS), and the product groups for which these significant coefficients are recorded cover most sectors of manufacturing industry except Instrument Engineering, Electrical Engineering and the Vehicle and Other Metal Goods industries.

In equation 9 certain product groups record significant coefficients with QQQQQQ and QQQQWS on XXIPOP, namely product groups 39, 46, 47, 71, 82, and 84, all of which have negative signs, and product groups 76, 78 and 79 with positive signs. Again therefore external diseconomies of scale seem to be existing where significant results occur, although it is possible that those product groups with negative coefficients require a professionally orientated labour force. Product groups 47 and 82 also record significant and negative coefficients on

XXIPOP with EFFINN.

In equation 10 there are fewer significant coefficients which are negative on SKLXXI than on LNXXXI and XXIPOP in equations 8 and 9, but little consistency of sign and significance on SKLXXI in the individual product groups with the three dependent variables. In product group 74 SKLXXI is positive and significant with each performance variable, whilst in product groups 76 and 79 it is negative and significant. No other product groups record consistent regression results on this variable with QQQQWS, QQQQQQ and EFFINN. Often the signs on the significant coefficients are different, as happens between QQQQWS and EFFINN in product groups 39 and 40, and between QQQQQQ and QQQQWS in product groups 23 and 83. Product group 46 (Domestic Electrical Goods) however records a positive coefficient on SKLXXI, significant at the 1% level with QQQQQQ and QQQQWS.

3 CONCLUSION

This chapter and the previous chapter have described, discussed and analysed the results of the regression analyses which were employed to test the validity of a number of hypotheses relating the performance of manufacturing industry to the existence of internal and external economies of scale. It has also permitted further study of the proxy variables which have been used as surrogates for the economy of scale effects being modelled.

The results show that generalisations about the operation of groups of product groups and whole sectors of manufacturing industry are likely to be misleading, and that ideally theperformance of each product group should be considered individually in relation to the implications of both internal and external economies of scale. In addition the dependent variable adopted to measure manufacturing performance is also an important factor in determining the significance of different proxy agglomeration variables, and of course this also varies by product group.

Notwithstanding these caveats, certain general conclusions can be drawn, without seriously distorting the results. Firstly, the size of plant variable recorded positive and significant coefficients in most product groups and with the majority of performance measures. Thus internal economies of scale do seem significant in general. The main exception is in the Electrical Engineering industry where no positive significant coefficients were recorded.

In relation to agglomeration factors, positive and significant effects were found to be most common when EFFINN was used as the dependent variable. The main exceptions were Chemicals, Electrical Engineering and Textiles, where insignificant or negative coefficients prevailed. With the other performance measures the most successful sectors were Food, Clothing, Bricks Pottery and Glass, Timber, and Paper Printing and Publishing. Product group 64 Hosiery, and 37 Industrial Plant also recorded a large number of positive and significant coefficients in sectors not otherwise significantly influenced by agglomeration factors on a wide scale.

The independent variables themselves were each found to behave quite uniquely. Their success in recording significant coefficients varied both with product group and dependent variable. Overall, the proxy variables applied seem to have operated in line with *a priori* expectations. The regression analysis has tended to support the general conclusions of the correlation exercise that for certain types of manufacturing industry external economies of scale reflected in measures of the local subregional environment can positively and significantly influence performance.

10 Summary and conclusions

1 THE OBJECTIVES OF THE RESEARCH

The role and importance of local external economies of scale has long been an established part of the theory associated with urban and regional economies and particularly with various theories of industrial location. From an empirical viewpoint however, this is an area which for a variety of reasons has not been well researched. While the arguments supporting the significance of local external economies are strong on a priori grounds, the evidence is limited and often inconclusive and contradictory as seen in the review in chapter three. This study has had the benefit of a data set not before available for analysis in the United Kingdom and has therefore permitted a new approach to discovering the significance of local external economies for British manufacturing industry.

The research has concentrated on analysing those externalities for manufacturing industry which are spatially determined and which are commonly referred to in the literature as 'economies of agglomeration'. This has involved deriving measures of those local influences upon industrial costs, progress and efficiency which result from the spatial juxtaposition of different industrial processes, suppliers, services, and customers, all of whom operate outside the control of the individual plant but nevertheless have the potential to influence the performance of that plant.

Previous research into the pattern and role of economies of agglomeration has tended to concentrate on analysing links between different industries and different industrial plants, both old and new. This is because local linkage has been identified with the existence of external economies, implying that external economies accrue to the industries or plants under study. There have been far fewer attempts to take this research one step forward to understand exactly what these links really mean for the industries concerned, and to associate characteristics of a local environment with measures of industrial performance. This study represents a step in this direction.

The study uses data from the 1968 Census of Production, provided in subregional form by manufacturing product group for net output per head, the average number of employees per establishment, the net output per establishment, and wages and salaries as a proportion of net output. From this information it has been possible to derive three different measures of industrial performance; net output per head, net output per head minus wages and salaries, and an efficiency index. The research has concentrated upon analysing the spatial distribution of these three performance measures and their statistical relationship with both internal and external economies of scale for fifty-three product groups in manufacturing industry in Great Britain. Insufficient observations prevented the study of a further twenty-six product groups.

The variables used to measure internal and external economies of scale were taken from a number of different sources including the Census of Production. No exact variables were available to measure perfectly the concepts being studied and a large number of proxy variables were tested in an attempt to derive the 'best' measures of agglomeration factors under review. These variables covered nearly forty different subregional economic and social characteristics.

It has been possible to identify both a number of proxy variables for measuring agglomeration economies and those manufacturing product groups for which particular agglomeration factors have both positive and negative significant effects on performance. In addition other product groups have been identified which seem to operate quite independently of location considerations, i.e. for which agglomeration effects are not significantly related to performance.

2 MAJOR RESEARCH PROBLEMS

There were a number of specific research problems which are relevant to the interpretation of the results. Firstly it should be remembered that three net output measures of performance were used in this project as indicators of relative productivity. Net output as defined in the Census of Production includes elements of services bought in from other companies and institutions outside the firm and outside the manufacturing sector. These items are normally excluded from the generally accepted concept used to measure productivity, namely value added.

Secondly, the subregions of Great Britain which formed the spatial basis for the research undertaken are not ideal for testing the hypotheses under consideration. They are defined on the basis of grouped administrative areas and therefore do not have functional boundaries from urban/rural/local economy aspects. They also differ considerably in size.

The net output data provided by the Census of Production by product group and by subregion is highly aggregated. Large and small and multiplant firms are collapsed into the same subregional average. The size distributions within each subregion are not known and the product groups vary greatly in the homogeneity of their outputs.

In addition, the number of subregional observations for each of the main data heads provided by the Census varies by product group. This was due to confidentiality and disclosure problems in cases where only a very few establishments were operating within any particular subregion.

Finally, in the regression estimations the relationships being explored between variables were, except for a number of logarithmic transformations, mainly of a linear form. The results did not appear to justify experimentation with more complex functions, although this is perhaps an area for future experimentation.

3 A SUMMARY OF THE PRINCIPAL CORRELATION RESULTS

Chapter seven was devoted to testing a wide range of alternative proxy variables for agglomeration economies using correlation analysis. Correlation coefficients were used to test the significance of relationships between the dependent performance variables and the wide variety of independent proxy variables, and also between the independent variables themselves.

(a) Internal economies of scale

Three different plant size variables were used to approximate the effect of internal economies of scale on performance. These were net output per establishment (NNNNQQ), the log of net output per establishment (LNNNQQ) and the average number of employees per establishment (NNNNLL). These variables were all highly intercorrelated but LNNNQQ recorded the largest number and most significant correlation coefficients of the three with the dependent variables. NNNNLL was the least successful of all. LNNNQQ recorded positive and significant coefficients in over two thirds of the manufacturing product groups, with both QQQQQQ and QQQQWS as performance variables. Negative coefficients were only recorded in product groups 45, 48/49, 69 and 72, and only in product group 45, Radio and Radar was a negative and significant relationship between plant size and performance found to exist.

Overall, therefore, these results suggest that size of plant is highly correlated with performance and that internal economies of scale are significant in manufacturing industry in general. Those product groups for which significant coefficients were not recorded (one third in all) came from a number of different industrial sectors but particularly Engineering and Clothing.

(b) External economies of scale

Although nearly forty different variables were experimented with it was only found possible to make any progress with the measurement of urbanisation effects. Two variables (size of industry in subregion, index of local market potential) were used in an attempt to measure the effect of localisation economies for individual manufacturing product groups but the results were not encouraging, and the variables were not used in the regression analysis.

Five different groups of urbanisation proxy variables were chosen, each group comprising a number of variables which were expected to measure similar agglomeration effects. It was anticipated that agglomeration effects would differ and also be identifiable and quantifiable according to:

1 Size of the subregion

2 Size and character of the manufacturing labour force in the subregion

3 Availability of service industry in the subregion.

4 Growth in the availability of services in the subregion.

5 Urban/rural character of the subregion.

The groups of variables chosen to reflect these five different agglomeration impacts were found in practice to overlap in their effects. In particular the size of subregion measured by such variables as urban population density, population and the average radius, was found to be highly intercorrelated with both the labour force and service industry availability variables and the size variables were therefore excluded from the regression analysis. Equally, the change in availability of services variable, although moderately successful in terms of recording significant coefficients positively related to manufacturing performance, was not chosen for use in the regression estimations because of the intention to use only cross sectional data representing conditions in the subregions in 1968 (or as close as possible).

The labour force variables were introduced to measure the availability and the skill level of the manufacturing workforce. Twelve different labour force variables were tested and many of these were intercorrelated, especially those measured in absolute numbers such as the numbers of employees in manufacturing, the numbers of skilled manufacturing employees and the numbers of economically active all reflecting size. Those which were less intercorrelated included male and female earnings, female activity rate, and the unemployment rate variables. With these variables and the dependent performance variables, significant correlation coefficients were widely distributed across product groups and tended to vary with the dependent variables. The unemployment rate produced mainly negative and significant correlation coefficients in a wide range of product groups representing most manufacturing sectors. This variable was therefore assumed to be acting as a proxy for the age and vitality of the different subregional economies and not as a labour availability variable. The number of unemployed however recorded positive coefficients and appeared to be a measure of the availability of labour.

The availability of services for manufacturing industry was measured by employment totals in eight selected service sectors by subregion. These measures were all very size dominated and hence intercorrelated. The significant correlation coefficients with the manufacturing performance measures were however always positive and suggest that the availability of services does reflect as a potential external economy, particularly in product groups 4, 37, 50, 59, 64, 70, 72, 74, 80 and 81. The Drink, Chemical, Metal Manufacture and Engineering industries were found to be least influenced by the spatial proximity of service availability. The extent of intercorrelation between each of the individual service variables led to experimentation with a composite service availability variable represented by the first principal component of all the service variables. This was used in the regression estimations as a surrogate for availability of services in general to manufacturing industries.

The character of each subregion was also reflected in three further variables. The most satisfactory in terms of obtaining significant correlation coefficients with the performance measures and not obtaining significant correlation coefficients with the other independent variables was the urban-rural dummy variable. The migration variable and the administrative classification into urban and rural were not carried forward to the regressions.

The correlation exercise also suggested the need to test some additional agglomeration variables which were less absolutely size dominated. Proportional variables were therefore introduced to measure the relative strength of particular independent variables: the total employed in manufacturing was used as a proportion of the population of the subregion, whilst the number of skilled manual workers was used as a proportion of the total manufacturing workforce in the subregion. Both variables were used in the regression estimations.

Overall, therefore, the correlation exercise emphasised the significance of internal economies of scale to most manufacturing industry, and the importance of certain external economies of scale to particular product groups. 25% of all product groups representing many different industrial sectors however, failed to record more than one significant correlation coefficient on the proxy agglomeration economy variables, with each of the performance measures as the dependent variable.

4 A SUMMARY OF THE PRINCIPAL REGRESSION RESULTS

Chapters eight and nine described the results of the cross sectional regression analysis. This consisted of estimating thirty different equations (ten sets of independent variables and three different dependent variables) for each of the fifty-three product groups across sixty-one subregions in Great Britain, and in this way observed the effects of different agglomeration economies for different manufacturing product groups.

In the regression equations the strength of the internal economies of scale effect discovered in the correlation analysis was strongly endorsed. The size of plant variable used to measure internal economies of scale only rarely recorded significant and negative regression coefficients with performance. More commonly the coefficients were positive and significant at least at the 5% level with each of the dependent variables. The Electrical Engineering industry represented the only sector in which the internal economy variable was generally either insignificant or negatively related to performance. The results varied with the product group: Radio and Radar always recording negative significant coefficients at 1% whilst the other three product groups in the industry recorded insignificant coefficients.

Seven different agglomeration economy proxy variables were used in the regression estimations. These were each introduced separately into an equation along with the size of plant variable. Three further equations were also estimated using different groups of the same independent agglomeration proxy variables to test whether the agglomeration effects were complementary in their effect on the performance of each industry.

The significance of each agglomeration economy proxy variable chosen to the performance of manufacturing industry varied both by product group and with the dependent performance variable. As such it is difficult to summarise the results and say which agglomeration effect is more significant. However, the availability of services for manufacturing industry as measured by the principal component of the numbers employed in a selection of service industries, and the availability of skilled manual workers as measured by the proportion of skilled manual employees in the manufacturing labour force in each subregion were both found to be important. Each of these recorded positive and significant coefficients at 10% in over a third of all product groups on average. Each recorded very few negative significant coefficients. With the efficiency index used to measure performance both variables recorded significant and positive coefficients at 5% in over a third of all product groups on average. Each recorded very few negative significant coefficients. With the efficiency index used to measure performance both variables recorded significant and positive coefficients at 5% in over half of the product groups and significant coefficients at 1% in nearly one quarter of all product groups. They represented the most successful agglomeration economy measures in terms of significant regression coefficients.

The variable used to measure the availability of labour in general and also to some extent the overall size of the agglomerations in each subregion was the number of employees in manufacturing industry. This variable was less successful than either the service availability or skilled worker availability variables but still recorded positive and significant coefficients at the 10% level in many of the product groups when performance was measured with the efficiency index. With net output per head minus wages and salaries measuring performance this labour force variable recorded significant negative coefficients as often as significant positive coefficients. It seems therefore that diseconomies of scale effects associated with measurement of the size of the agglomeration are being picked up by this variable. With net output per head significant coefficients on this labour force variable were generally positive.

Two of the agglomeration proxy variables recorded predominantly negative and significant regression coefficients. The unemployment rate, taken to be a measure of the age of capital and of the character and age of the industrial infrastructure in the subregion was negatively and significantly related to performance in approximately one third of all product groups. Again the greatest number of significant results was recorded with the efficiency index and the least with net output per head minus wages and salaries as the dependent variable.

The number of skilled manual workers in manufacturing as a proportion of the manufacturing workforce in total also tended to record negative and significant regression coefficients, suggesting that economies exist for certain manufacturing industries when the proportion of unskilled workers in the workforce increases. The strength and direction of this relationship tended, however, to vary with both the performance measures and the product groups. This variable recorded the least significant coefficients of all the independent variables used in the regression estimations.

The two remaining independent variables - URBRUR, an urban rural code and XXIPOP, the proportion of manufacturing employees in the population - were introduced to measure the character of the subregion and the relative availability of labour. Both produced a number of significant regression coefficients with positive and negative signs showing that large urban areas with relatively abundant supplies of labour are not necessarily conducive to maxmising manufacturing performance. Neither variable recorded significant regression coefficients with the same sign in any more than a fifth of all product groups with any particular dependent variable.

The regression results, as they relate to each product, can only be really considered individually since as already demonstrated they are apt to vary by product group, by dependent variable and by independent variable. At the risk of overgeneralising however, and hence possibly blurring certain issues, it is possible to make some broad conclusions.

Certain sectors of manufacturing industry seem to be influenced more in their performance than others by agglomeration economies, although in all cases the significance of results tends to vary with the dependent variable. The Food, Shipbuilding, Clothing, Bricks, Pottery, Glass, Timber and Paper Printing and Publishing industries generally seem to benefit from external economies of scale more than other sectors. Economies of agglomeration appear to have least impact on the performance of product groups in the Chemical industry, in Instrument and Electrical Engineering, and in the Textile industry with the exception of product group 64, Hosiery (which achieves a number of significant coefficients with many of the agglomeration economy variables, particularly LNXXXI, SKILMN and PCOMPI). There is finally a group of manufacturing sectors for which agglomeration economies are significant when performance is measured in one way and insignificant if it is measured in another. In the Drinks industry, in Metal Manufacturing, Mechanical Engineering, Vehicles, and Other Metal Goods agglomeration effects were of greatest significance when the efficiency index was used to measure performance. With net output per head minus wages and salaries, however, agglomeration factors had little significance. The extent of this difference is particularly marked in the Mechanical Engineering industry, although product group 37 (Industrial Plant) proved the exception being influenced positively by agglomeration factors however performance was measured.

Those individual product groups which stand out more than others as being significantly and positively influenced in their performance at the 10% level or more by a number of different agglomeration variables are product groups 4, 9, 37, 48/49, 64, 70, 73, 74, 76, 79, and 83. These product groups represent a wide range of manufacturing industry. Strong influences were also found in product groups 6, 26, 28, 34, 50, 52-55, 61, 68, 71, 72, 78, 80, 81 and 86.

Again it is difficult to generalise about which agglomeration factors are important for which sectors of manufacturing industry because the significance of each varies by product group and dependent variable. Very generally, service industry availability had greater significance on performance in the Clothing, Bricks, Pottery, Glass and Paper, Printing and Publishing sectors. The availability of skilled manual manufacturing workers assumed less importance in the Clothing industries but more in Food Manufacture. In addition, the absolute size of the manufacturing labour force used to measure labour availability was significantly and positively related to performance in a number of product groups in the Food manufacturing sector. It was also important in the Bricks Pottery and Glass and Paper Printing and Publishing sectors.

The relative availability of labour, the proportion of skilled manual labour in the manufacturing workforce, and the urban-rural index were not found to be consistently and significantly related to performance in any particular manufacturing sector. Instead the regression coefficients were sometimes positive, sometimes negative and varied in significance by product group and dependent variable. The age of capital variable produced mainly negative coefficients with all performance variables which were significant in many product groups representing all sectors of manufacturing industry except Drink, Electrical Engineering and Metal Goods.

Overall, the equations incorporating a number of independent agglomeration effects did not add substantially to the understanding of agglomeration processes. The results for each product group tended to only support the results of the less complex equations, although the age of capital, and the service availability variables each ended up recording significant regression coefficients in almost every product group in one of these equations or another. In addition, the urban-rural dummy tended to be more significant in combination with other agglomeration economy variables, and for a large number of product groups it suggested that rural locations were better than urban locations.

5 DIRECTIONS FOR FURTHER WORK

These results demonstrate time and again that it is probably misleading to talk in a broad and generalised way about agglomeration economies and their effect on the performance and location decisions of manufacturing industry. This analysis of the 1968 data shows clearly that agglomeration effects do exist but their influence is limited to specific product groups. Equally in these product groups some agglomeration economies seem to influence performance quite significantly no matter how that performance is measured, whilst in other cases a particular measure of performance is related to quite specific agglomeration effects.

These findings suggest that further research in this area is likely to be most profitable if it concentrates on specific industries. For example, in the Chemical, Instrument and Electrical Engineering industries and in much of the Textile industries, agglomeration economies do not seem important today. However in a number of specific product groups and also broad industrial sectors such as Food, Clothing, Timber Manufactures, Bricks Pottery and Glass, and Printing Paper and Publishing, research into the implications of agglomeration economies is likely to be rewarding. This would require individual industry surveys into the operations of firms within each industry on the basis of the selected products being manufactured.

Another area where further research seems both necessary and also feasible is in relation to economies of localisation. The size of industry in the subregion variable did seem to merit further investigation. In addition, subregional input-output data plant by plant would enable localisation effects to be measured more directly. The application of principal components analysis might also well be extended to more than just the service availability variables to include many of the other intercorrelated variables specific to an industry. In particular, the occupational mix of the labour pool in each area may be important in industries with very specialised labour skill requirements.

Finally there is also potential to introduce and experiment more with variables which represent change over time. Thus, for example, the agglomeration influences on changes in performance over time measured in terms of net output or even employment could be studied. Alternatively, change variables could also be introduced as independent variables as has been attempted here with the service employment variables.

It has been shown that the sources of economies of agglomeration are not only difficult to define but that they are also difficult to measure. Nevertheless the research has shown that some product groups operate more efficiently in urban areas and in particular types of urban areas; for others location is of little significance when seen in terms of agglomeration effects; and for other industries, rural locations are likely to be most advantageous for performance.

In each agglomeration of economic activity therefore a mix of potential externality influences exist and any one of these, independently or in combination, may or may not benefit a particular type of industry. This research has suggested broad areas of influence by product group and by different agglomeration economy effects. It is important that these issues are explored in more depth because they could have important implications for regional policy. Certain industries might, for example, be seen to operate most efficiently in inner cities, where perhaps service availability is at a premium, others in Development Areas or New Towns where particular skills or large labour pools are available. Some industries, as this study has shown, are not influenced in their locational choice by agglomeration factors, while rural locations offer advantages for others. Such findings are of importance not only for regional policy makers but also for local authority industrial development officers and planning officials.

Bibliography

Aberg, Y., 'Regional Productivity Differences in Swedish Manufacturing', Regional and Urban Economics, 3(2), 1973, pp.131-155.

Alonso, W., 'The Economics of Urban Size', Papers of the Regional Science Association, 27, 1970, pp.67-83.

Barr, J. L., 'City Size, Land Rent and the Supply of Public Goods', Regional and Urban Economics, 2, 1972, pp.67-103.

Baumol, W. J., 'Macro-economics of Unbalanced Growth: the Anatomy of Urban Crisis', American Economic Review, 57, 1967, pp.415-426.

Bergsman, J., Greenston, P. and Healy, R., 'The Agglomeration Process in Urban Growth', Urban Studies, 9, 1972, pp.263-288.

Bergsman, J., Greenston, P. and Healy, R., 'A Classification of Economic Activities Based on Location Patterns', Journal of Urban Economics, 2, 1975, pp.1-28.

Berry, B. J. L. and Gillard, Q., The Changing Shape of Metropolitan America: Commuting Patterns, Urban Fields and Decentralization Processes 1960-70, Ballinger, Cambridge, Massachusetts, 1977.

Bos, H. C., The Spatial Dispersion of Economic Activity, Rotterdam University Press, 1965.

Bosworth, D. L., Production Functions. A Theoretical and Empirical Study, Saxon House, Farnborough, Hampshire, 1976.

Britton, J. N. H., 'Environmental adaption of industrial plants: service linkages, locational environment and organization', in Hamilton, F. E. I. (ed), Spatial Perspectives on Industrial Organization and Decision Making, John Wiley, New York, 1974.

Brown, A. J., The Framework of Regional Economics in the United Kingdom, Cambridge University Press, London, 1972.

Bull, P. J., 'The Spatial Components of Intra-Urban Manufacturing Change: Suburbanization in Clydeside 1958-68', Transactions of the Institute of British Geographers, New Series, 3 (1), 1978, pp.92-100.

Burrows, J. C., Metcalf, C. E. and Kaler, J. B., Industrial Location in the United States, D. C. Heath, Lexington, Massachusetts, 1971.

Cameron, G. C. and Johnson, K. M., 'Comprehensive urban renewal and industrial relocation - the Glasgow case' in Cullingworth, J. B. and Orr, S. C. (eds), Regional and Urban Studies, Allen and Unwin, London, 1969.

Carlino, G. A., Economies of Scale in Manufacturing Location, Studies in Applied Regional Science, Vol. 12, Nijhoff, Leiden, 1979.

Central Statistical Office, Abstract of Regional Statistics, H.M.S.O., London, 1979.

Central Statistical Office, Regional Statistics, 14, H.M.S.O., London, 1979.

Chisholm, M. and Oeppen, J., The Changing Pattern of Employment: Regional Specialisation and Industrial Localisation in Britain, Croom Helm, London, 1973.

Crum, R. and Gudgin, G., Non Production Activities in U.K. Manufacturing Industry, Regional Policy Series No. 3, Commision of the European Communities, Brussels, 1977.

Creamer, D., 'Changing Location of Manufacturing Employment', Studies in Business Economics, No. 83, National Industrial Conference Board: New York, 1963.
Denison, E. F., Why Growth Rates Differ: Post-War Experience in Nine Western Countries, Brooking Institution, Washington, D.C., 1967.
Department of Trade and Industry, 'Inquiry into Location Attitudes and Experience', Memorandum Submitted to the Expenditure Committee (Trade and Industry Sub-Committee) on Regional Development Incentives, (Session 1973-1974, pp.525-668), H.C. 85-I, H.M.S.O., 1973.
Dixon, R. J. and Thirlwall, A. P., Regional Growth and Unemployment in the United Kingdom, Macmillan, London, 1975.
Drewett, R., Goddard, J. and Spence, J., British Cities: Urban Population and Employment Trends 1951-71, Research Report 10, Department of the Environment, London, 1976.
Economic Consultants Ltd., Strategic Plan for the South East, Studies Volume 5, H.M.S.O., London, 1971.
Edel, M., 'Land values and the costs of the urban congestion: measurement and distribution', in Ecole Paratiques des Hautes Etudes, Political Economy of Environment: Problems of Method, Mouton, The Hague, 1972.
Farrell, M. J., 'The Measurement of Productive Efficiency', Journal of the Royal Statistical Society, 120 Series A, 1957.
Fisher, F. M., 'The Existence of Aggregate Production Functions', Econometrica, 37, 1969.
Florence, P. S., Investment, Location and Size of Plant, Routledge and Kegan Paul, London, 1948.
Fothergill, S. and Gudgin, G., Regional Employment Change: A Sub-Regional Explanation, Progress in Planning, 12(3), Pergamon, Oxford, 1979.
Fuchs, V. R., Differentials in Hourly Earnings by Region and City Size, Occasional Paper No. 101, National Bureau for Economic Research, Columbia University Press, New York, 1967.
Gripaios, P., 'Industrial Decline in London: An Examination of Its Causes', Urban Studies, 14 (2), 1977, pp.181-190.
Gripaios, P., 'The Closure of Firms in the Inner City: The South East London Case 1970-75', Regional Studies, 11 (1), 1977, pp.1-6.
Hamer, A. M., Industrial Exodus from the Central City, Lexington Books, Massachusetts, 1973.
Haren, C. A., 'Rural Industrial Growth in the 1960's', American Journal of Agricultural Economics, 52 (3), pp.431-7.
Harris, C. C. and Hopkins, F. E., Locational Analysis: An Inter-Regional Econometric Model of Agriculture, Mining, Manufacturing and Services, Lexington Books, Lexington, Massachusetts, 1972.
Harrison, B., Urban Economic Development: Suburbanization, Minority Opportunity and the Condition of the Central City, The Urban Institute: Washington D.C., 1974.
Heathfield, D., Production Functions, Macmillan, London, 1971.
Hoare, A. G., 'Linkage Flows, Locational Evaluation and Industrial Geography: A Case Study of Greater London', Environment and Planning, 7, 1975, pp.41-58.
Hoch, I., 'Income and City Size', Urban Studies, 9, 1972, pp.299-328.

Hoover, E. M., The Location of Economic Activity, McGraw Hill, New York, 1948.
Isard, W., Location and Space Economy, M.I.T. Press, Cambridge, Massachusetts, 1956.
Jacobs, J., The Economy of Cities, Cape, London, 1970.
James, F. J. and Hughes, J. W., 'The Process of Employment Location Change: An Empirical Analysis', Land Economics, 69(4), 1973, pp.404-413.
Kain, J. F., 'Housing market discrimination and negro employment', chapter eight in Essays on Urban Spatial Structure, Ballinger, Cambridge, Massachusetts, 1975.
Kawashima, T., 'Urban agglomeration economies in manufacturing industries', Papers of the Regional Science Association, 34, 1975, pp.157-175.
Keeble, D. E., 'Industrial Migration from North West London, 1940-1964', Urban Studies, 2(1), 1965.
Keeble, D. E., 'Industrial Decentralisation and the Metropolis: The North West London Case', Transactions of the Institute of British Geographers, 44, pp.1-54.
Keeble, D. E., 'Local Industrial Linkage and Manufacturing Growth in Outer London', Town Planning Review, 40 (2), 1969, pp.163-188.
Keeble, D. E., 'Industrial Movement and Regional Development in the United Kingdom', Town Planning Review, 43 (10, 1972.
Keeble, D. E., Industrial Location and Planning in Britain, Methuen, London, 1976.
Keeble, D. E., 'Manufacturing dispersion and government policy in a declining industrial system: the United Kingdom case 1971-76', in Rees, J. et al., (eds), Industrial Systems and Regional Development, Croom Helm, 1980.
Keeble, D. E. and Hauser, D. P., 'Spatial Analysis of Manufacturing Growth in Outer South East England 1960-1967, I. Hypotheses and Variables', Regional Studies, 5, 1971, pp.229-262.
Keeble, D. E. and Hauser, D. P., 'Spatial Analysis of Manufacturing Growth in Outer South East England 1960-1967, II. Methods and Results', Regional Studies, 6, 1972, pp.11-36.
Kendrick, J. W., Productivity Trends in the United States, National Bureau for Economic Research, New York, 1961.
Laos, E. H. The Sources of Regional Differences in Efficiency: The Case of Mexican Manufacturing, Ph.D. Thesis, University of East Anglia, Norwich, 1977.
Lever, W. F., 'Industrial Movement, Spatial Association and Functional Linkages', Regional Studies, 6(4), 1972, pp.371-384.
Lever, W. F., 'Manufacturing linkages and the search for suppliers and markets', in Hamilton, F. E. I., (ed), Spatial Perspectives on Industrial Organisation and Decision Making, John Wiley, London, 1974.
Lever, W. F., 'Mobile Industry and Levels of Integration in Sub-Regional Economic Structures, Regional Studies, 9(3), 1975, pp.265-278.
Lever, W. F., 'Manufacturing decentralisation and shifts in factor costs and external economies', in Collins, L. and Walker, D. F., Location Dynamics of Manufacturing Industry, Wiley, London, 1975.
Lloyd, P. E. and Dicken, P., Location in Space: A Theoretical Approach to Economic Geography, Harper and Row, New York, 1977.
Lösch, A., The Economics of Location, Yale University Press, New Haven, Connecticut, 1954.

McCarthy, K. F. and Morrison, P. A., 'The Changing Demographic and Economic Structure of Non Metropolitan Areas in the 1970's', Rand Paper, p.6062, Santa Monica, California, 1978.
McCrone, G., Regional Policy in Britain, Allen and Unwin, London, 1969.
McDermott, P. J., 'Ownership, Organisation and Regional Dependence in the Scottish Electronics Industry', Regional Studies, 10, 1976, pp.319-335.
Mills, E. S., Studies in the Structure of the Urban Economy, John Hopkins Press, Baltimore, 1972.
Mitchell, A., 'Measuring Value Added from the Census of Production', Statistical News, 41, 1978, pp.4-9.
Moseley, M. J. and Townroe, P. M., 'Linkage Adjustment Following Industrial Movement', Tijdschrift voor Economische en Sociale Geografie, 64 (3), 1973, pp.137-144.
Pratten, C. F., Economies of Scale in Manufacturing Industry, Cambridge University Press, London, 1971.
Pred, A. R., The Spatial Dynamics of U.S. Urban-Industrial Growth 1800-1914, M.I.T. Press, Cambridge, Massachusetts, 1966.
Pred, A. R., 'On the Spatial Structure of Organisations and the Complexity of Metropolitan Interdependence', Papers of the Regional Science Association, 33, 1975, pp.115-142.
Pred, A. R., 'The Interurban Transmission of Growth in Advanced Economies: Empirical Findings Versus Regional Planning Assumptions', Regional Studies, 10 (2), 1976, pp.151-172.
Richardson, H. W., Regional Growth Theory, Macmillan, London, 1973.
Richardson, H. W., 'Empirical Aspects of Regional Growth in the United States', Annals of Regional Science, 8(2), 1974, pp.8-23.
Richter, C. E., 'The Inpact of Industrial Linkages on Geographic Association', Journal of Regional Science, 9(1), 1969, pp.19-28.
Sant, M. E. C., Industrial Movement and Regional Development: The British Case, Pergamon Press, Oxford, 1975.
Schmenner, R. W., The Manufacturing Location Decision: Evidence from Cincinnati and New England, Economic Development Research Report, U.S. Dept. of Commerce, Washington, D.C., 1978.
Segal, D., 'Are There Returns to Scale in City Size?', Review of Economics and Statistics, 58, 1976, pp.339-350.
Segal, M., Wages in the Metropolis: Their Influence on the Location of Industries in the New York Region, Harvard University Press, Cambridge, Massachusetts, 1960.
Shefer, D., 'Localisation Economies in S.M.S.A.'s: A Production Function Analysis', Journal of Regional Science, 13, pp.55-64.
Stanbach, T. M. and Knight, R. V., The Metropolitan Economy: The Process of Employment Expansion, Columbia University Press: New York, 1970.
Stone, D. N., Industrial Location in Metropolitan Areas: A General Model Tested for Boston, Praeger, New York, 1974.
Streit, M. E., 'Spatial Associations and Economic Linkages Between Industries', Journal of Regional Science, 9(2), 1969, pp.117-189.
Struyk, J. and James, F. R., Intra Metropolitan Industrial Location, Lexington Books, Lexington, Massachusetts, 1975.
Sveikauskas, L., 'The Productivity of Cities', Quarterly Journal of Economics, 89, 1975, pp.393-413.

Townroe, P. M., 'Locational Choice and the Individual Firm', Regional Studies, 3(1), 1969, pp.15-24.
Townroe, P. M., 'Industrial Linkage, Agglomeration and External Economies', Journal of the Town Planning Institute, 56(1), 1970, pp.18-20.
Townroe, P. M., Industrial Location Decisions: A Study in Management Behaviour, Occasional Paper No. 15, Centre for Urban and Regional Studies, University of Birmingham, 1971.
Townroe, P. M., 'Externalities for manufacturing industry in British subregions', in Breheny, M. J., (ed), Developments in Urban and Regional Analysis, London Papers in Regional Science 10, Pion, London, 1979.
Townroe, P. M., Industrial Movement: Experience in the U.S. and U.K., Saxon House, Farnborough, Hants., 1979.
Vining, D. R. and Kontuly, L., 'Population Dispersal from Major Metropolitan Regions: An International Comparison', International Regional Science Review, 3, pp.49-73.
Walters, A. A., 'Production and Cost Functions: An Econometric Survey', Econometrica, 31, 1963.
Webber, M. J., Impact of Uncertainty on Location, M.I.T. Press, Cambridge, Massachusetts, 1972.
Weber, A., Theory of the Location of Industries, translated by Friedrich, C. I., University of Chicago Press, Chicago, 1929.
Wheat, L. F., Regional Economic Growth and Industrial Location, D. C. Heath, Lexington, Massachusetts, 1973.
Wood, P. A., 'Industrial Location and Linkage', Area, 1, 1969, 32-39.

Index